JAMESON'S MEN

The Story of the Jameson Raid

1895 – 96

WITH

BRITISH SOUTH AFRICA POLICE BANNERS,

BATTLE HONOURS AND MEMORIALS

C.E. ROGERS (4735)

TSL Publications

The Great War in Africa Association

First published by the British South Africa Police Regimental
Association (United Kingdom Branch) 2013.

Published in Great Britain in 2024

By Great War in Africa Association, TSL Publications,
Rickmansworth

ISBN: 978-1-917426-09-1

Apology is made for the standard of some photographs. This is
caused by scanning from old magazines with poor paper quality.

Language has been retained for historical reasons.

Acknowledgements:
See the Author's acknowledgement of assistance of B. Taylor
(5507), G. Quick (6682) and J. Sutton (8725) in his
Introduction.
References to various official documents in the Appendices.
History Section Committee, United Kingdom Branch, B.S.A.P.
Regimental Association, (Chairman Alan Toms).
The Bodleian Library, Oxford. See Map A2
Old faded maps have been enhanced as far as possible.
Initially edited and typeset by John Berry (5584)

CONTENTS

Abbreviations	5
Introduction	7
Setting the Scene	11
Tomlinson's Account	13
Sir John Willoughby's Report	18
The Pitsani Account	37
The Daily State	38
Force Strength	39
White's Diary	40
Spurious Claimants to Fame	41
Sir H. Robinson's Telegram/Report	43
Contemporary Accounts of the Raid List	45
Appendices	46
Nominal Roll/Service Records	55
Brief Note on Anglo-Boer War	95
B.S.A.P. Banners, Colours and Battle Honours, and Memorials	101

PHOTOGRAPHS/MAPS

Dr. Jameson and Sir John Willoughby	4
Maps	26 to 31
Prisoners at Volksrust railway goods yard	41
First trainload of prisoners	41
Dr. Jameson at Pretoria Gaol	42
Officers en-route to England	42
B.S.A.P. Squadron, 1900	95
Armoured Train in Bulawayo	96
Imperial Bushmen Maxim Company	100
The 1904 Banner	102
Colour Party	119
Colour Party, 1907	120
Cavalry Memorial, London	122
Blatherwick Memorial	124
B.S.A.P. Memorial, National Memorial Arboretum	125-129
Roll of Honour	129
Centenary Plaque	130
Shangani Memorial, Scotland	131

Leander Starr Jameson
Instigator of the Raid

ABBREVIATIONS

B.B.P.	Bechuanaland Border Police.
Bel.Col.	Belingwe Column.
B.F.F.	Bulawayo Field Force.
B.S.A.P.	British South Africa Police.
B.S.A.C.P.	British South Africa Company Police.
CinC. BG.	C. in C.'s Bodyguard.
C.M.R.	Cape Mounted Rifles.
C.P.	Cape Police.
Dow.	Died of wounds.
Dws.	Died while serving.
H.C.	SS *Harlech Castle*.
Kia.	Killed in action.
M.H.	Mashonaland Horse.
M.M.P.	Mashonaland/Matabeleland Mounted Police.
M.R.F.	Matabeleland Relief Force.
Mia.	Missing in action.
Mt.Dar. Vols.	Mount Darwin Volunteers.
N.M.R.	Natal Mounted Rifles.
Rh.F.F.	Rhodesian Field Force.
R.H.V.	Rhodesian Horse Volunteers.
R.C.	SS *Roslin Castle*.
R.R.	Rhodesia Regiment.
S.F.F.	Salisbury Field Force.
S.A.C.	South African Constabulary.
S.R.Col.	Southern Rhodesia Column. (G.E.A.).
SRC.	Southern Rhodesia Constabulary.
S.R.V.	Southern Rhodesian Volunteers.
U.V.C.	Umtali Volunteer Column.
Vict.	SS *Victoria*.
Vic.Col.	Victoria Column.
W.A.F.F.	West African Frontier Force.
W.L.H.	Western Light Horse.
W.W.W.	Who Was Who & Vol.No.x

Sir John Willoughby
when second in command of the B.S.A.C.P.
Military commander of the Raid.

INTRODUCTION

Over the years that I have been interested in this subject I have accumulated various items of information that are of interest in themselves but not relevant to the main story and if I do not write them down now they will be lost. I trust they will be of interest.

The major source of information was the nominal roll of Jameson's Force repatriated by the British Authorities. The men were handed over to the British Army at Volksrust on the Natal Transvaal border on the 21st to 23rd January 1896 and were then conveyed to Durban and placed aboard ships that sailed from that port. The ships were the *Victoria* that sailed on the 21st January, the *Harlech Castle* and *Roslin Castle* that sailed on the 24th, the *Mexican* 1st February, *Dunnottar Castle* on the 8th, the *Illovo* on the 9th, the *Norman* on the 18th, the *Matabele* on the 21st, *Inanda* and *Pretoria* on the 14th March and the *Grantuilly Castle* on the 14th April 1896. The documents are the original hand written lists made at the time of the hand over and were copied as seen in a semi-alphabetical state. They are signed by the then Governor of Natal, Sir Walter Healy-Hutchinson.

Another important source has been the National Archives of Botswana where rolls compiled by the M.M.P. were located. These give the names of the members of the Force by troop and includes the missing and escapees filling gaps in the Volksrust List. These were prepared sometime after the raid and at the time of re-mustering at Mafeking prior to the men's return to Bulawayo. The above material is supported by the passenger manifests of the *Harlech Castle* but which lists only those repatriated to the United Kingdom. A, B, C, D and Artillery Troops were members of the Matabeleland Mounted Police, G & K Troops were recruited from members of the Bechuanaland Border Police.

As in all efforts to compile a list of this nature there will be errors and a variation in the spelling of names. The manner in which members were recruited and the short time they spent together make the task of compiling an accurate list of the men difficult. To this we must take into account the number of persons in the force who maybe did not want their whereabouts published and who may have given a different name, either on recruitment or capture. There can be no guarantee that the list is complete. To illustrate the manner of recruitment I have included extracts from Robert White's Diary where he notes the arrival of recruits and potential recruits into the camp before the raid. This diary was introduced in evidence at the Old

8

Bailey trial. I have been unable to locate the original Muster Rolls. The summary of the handover to the British Authorities also contains various anomalies. I also have the impression that the Transvaal authorities had only a scanty idea of the names and numbers involved.

There have been suggestions that the prisoners were badly treated while in the hands of their captors, I have never come across any reports of ill treatment. After repatriation some prisoners complained that they had lost valuable personal possessions and were seeking compensation for gold watches and other similar items taken from them by their captors. I have included a facsimile of a page from the *Critic*, a local paper published at the time in Johannesburg which shows the general tone of some of the press after the Raid. The evidence to support this story cannot be found, no officer was left unaccounted for and the report is unsupported by other first hand accounts written at the time by the men themselves. On the contrary, many men spoke about the fair manner in which they had been treated. There is a record in the Gaberone Archives of a Tpr. Martin Brown, M.M.P., who was alleged to have been captured and shot. The same man was reported killed in the action at Doornkop by two witnesses, Tomlinson and Gorringe.

We know that during the Anglo Boer War many of Jameson's Force became senior members of the South African Constabulary on its foundation in 1900, others were administrators in the South African Republic and the Free State when they were occupied. If there had been reports of this nature they would, I believe, have been fully investigated at this time. Nothing has been found to indicate that any such investigations took place.

On the roll the names with a number were shown on the Volksrust List, the names without numbers were obtained from the Gaberone Archive and other sources and is an attempt to fill the gap with the names of the escapees. The information contained on the list tries to list service prior to the raid and subsequent to the raid on the right. Beneath the troop letter is a number, this is the age of the person given on the Harlech Castle passenger manifest at the time travelling in January and February 1896.

Bechuanaland Border Police.
The B.B.P. ceased to be paid by the Imperial Government on the 15th December 1895, G and K Troops were taken on to the B.S.A. Com. Payroll later in December. They were still referred to as the B.B.P. for administration purposes and served in their existing troop formations. Technically the

B.B.P. did not participate in the Jameson Raid as they had been disbanded. The disbandment of the B.B.P. was due to the transfer of British Bechuanaland to the Cape, the police of that area, Troops A and B, were incorporated into the C.M.P.

Capture and handover.
After the members of Jameson's Force had been captured they were imprisoned and eventually transferred to Volksrust. There are doubts as to whether the Boers had an accurate record of the persons they had captured with the exception of the main participants and the first attempt at an accurate record seems to have been compiled by the British Army at the time of the hand over on the 23rd January 1896. I have not been able to trace a copy of this roll in the War Office files but one was located in the Colonial Office files of the period. Various reports give a differing number as to the composition of the force. It is doubtful if full records will ever be found. Men were recruited into the M.M.P. at Pitsani who had never been to Matabeleland and may never have travelled there after the raid. Although before disembarking in England the men were informed that they were still under contract and were expected to adhere to this contract some did not return. I doubt whether this contract would have been enforceable considering the circumstances.

Transport and Repatriation.
The prisoners, as they had become, were transported in two trains from Charlestown to Durban. The journey was supposed to be nonstop and the blinds were to be kept down in the windows to avoid contact with the civilian populace as they passed through the stations en route. These instructions were flouted and as they progressed to the coast the men were feted in almost every station as they passed on their way. On arrival in Durban they were detrained and taken immediately to a lighter and then aboard the *Harlech Castle*. The ship was then instructed to sail directly to England, avoiding all ports until arrival there, as a result of this instruction 103 officers and men had to be offloaded to the *Roslyn Castle* which would deliver them to East London, Port Elizabeth and Cape Town. The records show that 8 other ranks were off loaded in Durban, 2 officers and 27 other ranks in East London, 33 other ranks in Port Elizabeth and 1 officer and 32 other ranks in Cape Town. The embarrassment the Raid had caused the Imperial Government also involved much expense. The *Harlech Castle* charter cost £5000 sterling and the *Roslyn Castle* £1200. This money was repaid to the government by the B.S.A. Co. without much arm twisting as at

the time there were moves afoot in England to strip the company of its Charter. As most of the men had lost most of their personal kit and they would be arriving in England in the depth of winter they had to be clothed.

Local tailors were contracted to outfit each man with a topcoat, jacket, trousers, shirts, etc. This issue was most likely paid for by the B.S.A.Co. One outcome of this transport arrangement was a passenger list, a requirement for all ships carrying passengers and arriving in a British port from about 1860 onwards. This information complements the Volksrust Roll and gives one additional piece of information, the age of the passenger. The authorities obviously had not made up their minds on how the situation was to be handled after the arrival of the *Harlech Castle* in England. The captain was informed that he should proceed slowly to delay his arrival. On arrival at Plymouth, England, the prisoners were released from custody, placed on a special train and taken to Paddington where they were free to disperse to their final destinations.

Prosecution of Officers.

Only the officers on the staff were prosecuted for their involvement in the venture, the papers of this prosecution are in the public domain. The names of the witnesses called for the prosecution, including members of the M.M.P. and various exhibits introduced at the trial make interesting reading.

This account is an effort to list the names of the men who took part in the Jameson Raid into the Transvaal late December early January 1895-96, the political aspects of the Raid have been well covered by various authors over the years but I do not know of a publication naming the participants. This is a revision of material first published in 2002. Once again I must express my thanks for the support and assistance I had from other people. To mention a few; Brian Taylor, Geoff Quick and John Sutton. Where known all sources are acknowledged. The opinions expressed and errors are down to me alone.

C.E. Rogers (4735)
Petersfield, July 2012

SETTING THE SCENE FOR THE RAID

Extract from Origins and Early History of the B.S.A.P. *by W.B. Bussy (exTrooper no.1084).*

The prologue of the drama which we know as the Jameson Raid has been described most vividly by an eyewitness. The story is absolutely authentic:

The scene is the stoep of Government House, Bulawayo. The leading actor is His Honour Leander Starr Jameson, M.D., C.B., Administrator of Matabeleland. The time is one of great unrest, with tales of oppression and injustice pouring all over the Empire from the mouths and pens of the large body of Britishers who labour in the gold mines around Johannesburg. The Imperialist papers, British and South African, are crying aloud their complaints and remedies, and but a slight touch of the torch is wanting to set the pile of discontent alight. The doctor has in his hands a cigarette which he is smoking, and a *Life of Clive* which he reads attentively. Suddenly he looks up from the book and exclaims: 'I have a jolly good mind to march straight down the plateau with the men I have here, and settle the thing out of hand. The idea of South Africa going on being trodden upon by this Pretoria gang is absurd. I have a good mind to get the fellows together and start tomorrow, via Tati.'

A companion suggests that there are, at the most, a couple of hundred Matabeleland Mounted Police available, that it would take them at least three weeks to carry out the proposed programme, and that meanwhile the international situation would be somewhat peculiar, probably resulting in the disbandment of the regiment by cable.

'You may say what you like,' says the man of action, 'but Clive would have done it.' That seems to be the origin of the whole muddle and mystery of the Raid: 'Clive would have done it.'

The original plan of the would-be revolutionists was as follows: The British party in Johannesburg was to form an ultimatum and follow it up by force sufficient to take the town and declare itself a Provisional Government. The same night a surprise visit to Pretoria was to be made, and the final coup accomplished without firing a shot. Downing Street had already been sounded as to its probable actions, but the malcontents had been assured that Great Britain could not interfere in the internal affairs of the Transvaal on their behalf, and could only act afterwards by way of keeping the peace in South Africa, and not at a time or in a way which could be construed as assisting to break it. Hence the border was looked to.

THE JAMESON RAID

By: Lt.-Col. A.J.T. Tomlinson, B.S.A.P.

There were twenty-six of the police who started from Salisbury in September 1895, for the march to Bulawayo under Sub-Inspector Charles Southey. In those days the ranks of inspector and sub-inspector were equivalent to captain and lieutenant, and the police were known as the M.M.P., Mashonaland and Matabeleland Mounted Police. Our uniform was a dark greyish cord tunic and breeches, with black field boots and slouch hat, the brim turned up on one side, with the badge affixed.

The roads were mere tracks and we had no wheeled transport with us, the rear of the detachment bringing along led pack horses, which carried blankets and packbags. Meals were obtained on requisition from wayside stores which were not too numerous, so our feeding hours were not regular. Of course we had no idea that we were off to take part in the Jameson Raid. Only two police stations were passed on the road, Fort Charter (Enkeldoom way) near what is known as the farm Marshbrook, and Gwelo, then outside the small township. When we arrived at Bulawayo our detachment formed part of C Troop. There were no squadrons then. Three officers went to a troop, the two sub-inspectors having charge of half-troops. Shortly after arriving at Bulawayo I was promoted to sub-inspector and was posted to D Troop under Inspector Dykes.

Our march through Botswana began soon after, A Troop under Inspector Straker starting first, the others following at intervals of a few days until Pitsani was reached (Pitsani Pothlugu, to give it its full name) situated quite close to the Transvaal border. Here our camp was formed, and parades and other duties of a military force followed day in and day out. We were about 400 strong, with a 12½ pounder and six maxims, Lieutenant-Colonel Bodle being Commanding Officer. Still no word of why all this was taking place – not a whisper – but rumour had it that the native chief in the area was unruly, and the force was a necessary demonstration to him and his following.

There was a large Headquarters Staff including Dr. Jameson, Sir John Willoughby and Lieutenant-Colonel the Hon. Harry White, who was Commissioner M.M.P. On Sunday afternoon, the 29th of December 1895, a parade of all ranks was ordered without any preliminary warning, and Dr. Jameson came along (with all the staff) and addressed the troops. He gave a brief outline of how unfairly the Uitlanders were being treated by the

Transvaal Government, and went on to say that they had at last been driven to assert their rights. It was intended that our force was to proceed to Johannesburg to give our fellow-men assistance in their extremity. Any man who did not wish to take part in this venture was at liberty to step from the ranks. Not a single man took advantage of the chance of remaining behind; there were cheers and the parade was dismissed, followed by great excitement amongst all.

At 6.30 p.m. the same day the whole of the force assembled at Pitsani, soon after to cross into the Transvaal. We marched forty miles throughout the night, reaching Malmani soon after daybreak. Here on our arrival a force of the Bechuanaland Border Police of about 125 men with two 7-pounder guns and six maxims, under Lieutenant-Colonel Raleigh Grey, joined us.

We marched on without interruption, with occasional halts for rest and food until near midnight on 31st December, 1895, when the first skirmish with a small party of Transvaalers took place, and bullets whistled; but this did not last long. However, it made us realise there would be further fighting. Meals were irregular, my impression was that wayside stores had been arranged, which to the uninitiated were ordinary trading stores, but at these, tinned provisions, etc., were obtained for the force and were issued.

At Ottoshoop there was one such store, which we reached early on New Years Day, and here were fresh horses in a fenced paddock, and we were told to help ourselves and exchange them for our tired animals. But not a single horse of the new lot was rideable. They were all unbroken to bit and saddle. Someone must have reaped a harvest over this business deal.

By this time, with very little sleep for man or horse, our force was becoming tired out, but we pushed on for Krugersdorp. Somewhere about 11 a.m., 1st January 1896, two cyclists were met, who, we were told, had brought news that a column from Johannesburg would meet us near Krugersdorp, which was held by 300 Transvaalers. Before reaching Krugersdorp, a party of Zarps (Transvaal Mounted Troops) were seen in extended order, their blue uniforms showing up clearly in the bare veld. Our guns opened on them, and they were seen to scatter and retire.

The vicinity of Krugersdorp was reached at about 4.30 p.m., and after some waiting, was shelled by our artillery, but this brought no return of fire from the garrison. We reconnoitred D Troop to the left, but our advance was quickly stopped by a withering fire from rifle pits. We retired with some casualties. I remember one horse, with saddle empty, galloping with us.

Night was coming on and the column then headed half-right, and in the darkness formed into a hollow square, as near as might be, a mile or two beyond. I was detailed to take out some men to form sentry posts, and while engaged in this duty came in for fire from the Transvaalers, which was promptly replied to from our force. Luckily there was an opportune fold in the ground, which saved us under the cross fire. The spasmodic attack was soon over, and then I took the men in, shouting 'Friends' as we approached our lines, knowing that it was useless to remain beyond our lines. We were attacked three times during the night, and as it grew light found our bivouac was near the railway embankment, from which the Transvaalers could fire from cover.

Then the column moved by successive troops at the gallop pretty well over a ridge, two troops (of which D was one) fighting a rear-guard action. Just before we moved off in the coming daylight I remember seeing Corporals Still and Beard had met their end, and a man named Brown who had been transferred from the town police at Bulawayo, whom I turned over because I thought he was still asleep, was also dead, all D Troop members.

Our progress was slow, the Transvaalers keeping at long range, and gradually coming up on our flanks as we retired by alternate half troops in rear-guard action. We passed a place called Randfontem, where the British miners came out and cheered us. Trooper Bletsoe was killed soon after we passed Randfontein, and sometime later I saw in the press that the miners had buried him and subscribed for a stone for his grave, which showed true sympathy in his unfortunate death. I remember one of the officers of the staff, Lieutenant Kincaid-Smith, losing his horse after operating one of the maxim guns, and as we were passing at the time he got a lift with me on my horse to our wagons. He was most grateful.

Meantime heavy firing was taking place in front. We in the rear-guard action were gradually closing up, as further progress to Johannesburg was barred by about 800 Transvaalers in a safe position at Doornkop. Their machine-guns, arriving late, had just opened on us, when in the midst of the din of battle a trumpeter was seen to go forward with someone else holding a pole on which was a large piece of white cloth. The 'Cease fire' was sounded, faintly at first, but which became more pronounced as the firing began to die down. Then followed a stillness which was remarkable.

Batches of us gradually stood up and all wondered what would take place next.

The Transvaalers came riding down from the koppies after a time, and lined up, mounted, in the valley. Of course I knew nothing of what messages had passed between Dr. Jameson and the leaders of the Transvaal Burgher Force. Word was passed along to instruct the troops to assemble opposite the burghers. Gradually our force drifted in, leading the poor tired-out horses, and arms were laid on the ground. Officers were assembled where there was a farm house with a stone wall, some lying wounded; our artillery and machine-guns nearby.

Some hour or so elapsed, and our men then moved away under escort, with their horses. Officers were bundled into ox-wagons and eventually Krugersdorp was reached, and we were placed at the foot of Paardekraal monument. The men and horses were camped some little distance away.

Next morning all officers appeared before the magistrate, our names were taken and certain interrogations made, Sir John Willoughby (looking fearfully downhearted) replying.

Then ox-wagons again and we travelled to Pretoria, while our men marched under escort in front. Dr. Jameson was driven in a Cape cart. It was cold and my coloured boy, Frog, had lost my tunic; none of us had anything except what we stood in. Salvoes of rifle fire were indulged in by our captors as the procession neared the villages en route, and all inhabitants turned out to see the unusual sight.

At Pretoria our men were taken off to the race course, and a long wait ensued before the jail official would admit the officers into the jail precinct. Nearly thirty of us were crammed into small cells at night which in ordinary time would barely have accommodated a fourth of the number. Dr. Jameson was given a separate cell. There was a white line in front of the cells which gave the limit we were not allowed to go beyond. Food was wheeled to us in large tin buckets. And here we remained for over a week until the Reform Committee from Johannesburg was arrested and the members brought to the prison.

We were then removed to the grandstand at the race course. Then, after a few days we were sent by train to Volksrust, near the Natal border. For three weeks we were quartered in the wool sheds at the railway station, being allowed to bathe in batches in the running stream close by. Eventually, after some palaver with the Attorney-General from Natal and the Dutch officials, an escort of the 7th Hussars under Major Evans arrived with two trains, and all those for the British Isles were placed on board the S.S.*Harlech Castle* when we arrived at Durban. Here we were outfitted to a certain extent, tailors visiting the officers, but it was not divulged who paid the expenses!

The towns of Maritzburg and Durban wished to give us hospitality but this was not allowed.

We ended the voyage at Plymouth and two special trains took us to London. I shall never forget the tremendous crowd that met us on our arrival at Paddington. We were allowed to go where we chose as soon as we left the trains at London. The hansom cab that I got to take me to Victoria for Eastbourne took a long time to get clear.

The officers who had Imperial Commissions were sent home in the war vessel which took Dr. Jameson, and were tried with him at the Old Bailey.

I might just end by saying that the force travelled over 170 miles from Pitsani to Doornkop in eighty-six hours, the last seventeen of which saw almost continuous fighting. Of the M.M.P. we had Inspector Barry die of wounds and Sub-Inspector Cazalet wounded. If my memory serves me aright, of the British there were twenty-three killed and sixty-four wounded.

This article first appeared in The Outpost Regimental Magazine of the British South Africa Police *and subsequently in other publications.*

SIR JOHN WILLOUGHBY'S REPORT TO THE WAR OFFICE

Official Report of the Expedition That Left the Protectorate at the Urgent Request of the Leading Citizens of Johannesburg with the Object of Standing by Them and Maintaining Law and Order Whilst They Were Demanding Justice from the Transvaal Authorities. By Sir John C. Willoughby, Bart., Lieutenant-Colonel Commanding Dr. Jameson's Forces.

On Saturday, December 28, 1895, Dr. Jameson received a Reuters telegram showing that the situation at Johannesburg had become acute. At the same time reliable information was received that the Boers in the Zeerust and Lichtenburg districts were assembling, and had been summoned to march on Johannesburg.

Preparations were at once made to act on the terms of the letter dated December 20, and already published, and also in accordance with verbal arrangements with the signatories of that letter – viz., that should Dr. Jameson hear that the Boers were collecting, and that the intentions of the Johannesburg people had become generally known, he was at once to come to the aid of the latter with whatever force he had available, and without further reference to them, the object being that such force should reach Johannesburg without any conflict.

3 p.m. on Sunday afternoon, December 29, everything was in readiness at Pitsani Camp. The troops were paraded, and Dr. Jameson read the letter of invitation from Johannesburg.

He then explained to the force: (a) that no hostilities were intended; (b) that we should only fight if forced to do so in self-defence; (c) that neither the persons nor property of inhabitants of the Transvaal were to be molested; (d) that our sole object was to help our fellow-men in their extremity, and to ensure their obtaining attention to their just demands. Dr. Jameson's speech was received with the greatest enthusiasm by the men, who cheered most heartily. The above programme was strictly adhered to until the column was fired upon on the night of the 31st.

Many Boers, singly and in small parties, were encountered on the line of march; to one and all of these the pacific nature of the expedition was carefully explained.

The force left Pitsani Camp at 6.30 p.m., December 29, and marched through the night.

At 5.15 a.m. on the morning of the 30th the column reached the village of Malmani (39 miles distant from Pitsani).

Precisely at the same moment the advanced guard of the Mafeking Column (under Colonel Grey) reached the village, and the junction was effected between the two bodies.

For details of the composition of the combined force, as also for general particulars of the march to Krugersdorp, see sketch of the route and schedule attached (marked A. and B. respectively).

From Malmani I pushed on as rapidly as possible in order to cross in daylight the very dangerous defile at Lead Mines. This place, distant 71 miles from Pitsani, was passed at 5.30 p.m., December 30.

I was subsequently informed that a force of several hundred Boers, sent from Lichtenburg to intercept the force at this point, missed doing so by three hours only.

At our next 'off-saddle' Dr. Jameson received a letter from the Commandant-General of the Transvaal demanding to know the reason of our advance, and ordering us to return immediately. A reply was sent to this, explaining Dr. Jameson's reasons in the same terms as those used to the force at Pitsani.

At Doornport (91 miles from Pitsani), during an 'off-saddle' early on Tuesday morning, December 31, a mounted messenger overtook us, and presented a letter from the High Commissioner, which contained an order to Dr. Jameson and myself to return at once to Mafeking and Pitsani.

A retreat by now was out of the question, and to comply with these instructions an impossibility. In the first place, there was absolutely no food for men or horses along the road which we had recently followed; secondly, three days at least would be necessary for our horses, jaded with forced marching, to return; on the road ahead we were sure of finding, at all events, some food for man and beast. Furthermore, we had by now traversed almost two-thirds of the total distance; a large force of Boers was known to be intercepting our retreat, and we were convinced that any retrograde movement would bring on an attack of Boers from all sides.

It was felt, therefore, that to ensure the safety of our little force, no alternative remained but to push on to Krugersdorp to our friends, who we were confident would be awaiting our arrival there. Apart from the above considerations, even had it been possible to effect a retreat from Doornport, we knew that Johannesburg had risen, and felt that by turning back we should be shamefully deserting those coming to meet us.

Finally, it appeared to us impossible to turn back, in view of the fact that we had been urgently called in to avert a massacre, which we had been assured would be imminent in the event of a crisis such as had now occurred. Near Boon's store, on the evening of the 31st, an advanced patrol fell in with Lieutenant Eloff, of the Krugersdorp Volunteers. This officer, in charge of a party of 15 scouts, had come out to gain intelligence of our movements. He was detained whilst our intentions were fully explained to him, and then released at Dr. Jameson's request.

At midnight (New Years Eve), while the advanced scouts were crossing rocky wooded ridge at right angles to and barring the line of advance, they were fired on by a party of 40 Boers, who had posted themselves in this position. The scouts, reinforced by the advanced guard under Inspector Straker, drove off their assailants after a short skirmish, during which one trooper of the M.M.P. was wounded.

At Van Oudtshoorn's, early on the following morning (January 1), Dr. Jameson received a second letter from the High Commissioner, to which he replied in writing. At 9.30 a.m. the march was resumed in the usual day formation. After marching two miles, the column got clear of the hills and emerged into open country. About this time Inspector Drury, in command of the rearguard, sent word that a force of about 100 Boers was following him about one mile in rear. I thereupon reinforced the rearguard, hitherto consisting of a troop and one Maxim, by an additional half-troop and another Maxim.

11 a.m. About 5 miles beyond Van Oudtshoorn's store the column was met by two cyclists bearing letters from several leaders of the Johannesburg Reform Committee. These letters expressed the liveliest approval and delight at our speedy approach, and finally contained a renewal of their promise to meet the column with a force at Krugersdorp. {55} (sic) The messengers also reported that only 300 armed Boers were in the town. This news was communicated to the troops, who received it with loud cheers.

Then within two miles of Hinds store, the column was delayed by extensive wire-fencing, which ran for one and a half miles of either side of the road and practically constituted a defile.

While the column was halted and the wire being cut, the country for some distance on both sides was carefully scouted. By this means it was ascertained that there was a considerable force of Boers (1) on the left front, (2) in the immediate front (retreating hastily on Krugersdorp), (3) a third party on the right flank. The force which had been following the column from Van Oudtshoorn's continued to hover in the rear.

Lieutenant-Colonel White, in command of the advanced guard, sent back a request for guns to be pushed forward as a precaution in case of an attack from the Boers in front. By the time these guns reached the advanced guard, the Boers were still retreating some two miles off. A few rounds were then fired in their direction. Had Colonel White, in the first instance, opened fire with his Maxims on the Boers, whom he surprised watering their horses close to Hind's store, considerable loss would have been inflicted; but this was not our object, for with the exception of the small skirmish on the previous night, the Boers had not as yet molested the column, whose sole aim was to reach Johannesburg if possible without fighting.

At this hour Hinds store was reached. Here the troops rested for one and a half hours. Unfortunately, hardly any provisions for men and horses were available.

An officers' patrol, consisting of Major Villiers (Royal Horse Guards) and Lieutenant Grenfell (1st Life Guards) and six men, moved off for the purpose of reconnoitring the left flank of the Boer position, while Captain Lindsell, with his permanent force of advanced scouts, pushed on as usual to reconnoitre the approach by the main road. At the same time I forwarded a note to the Commandant of the forces in Krugersdorp to the effect that, in the event of my friendly force meeting with opposition on its approach, I should be forced to shell the town, and that therefore I gave him this warning in order that the women and children might be moved out of danger. To this note, which was despatched by a Boer who had been detained at Van Oudtshoorn, I received no reply.

At Hinds store we were informed that the force in our front had increased during the forenoon to about 800 men, of whom a large number were entrenched on the hillside.

Four miles beyond Hinds store, the column following the scouts, which met with no opposition, ascended a steep rise of some 400 feet, and came full in view of the Boer position on the opposite side of a deep valley, traversed by a broad 'sluit' or muddy water course. Standing on the plateau or spur, on which our force was forming up for action, the view to our front was as follows: Passing through our position to the west was the Hinds store – Krugersdorp Road traversing the valley and the Boer position almost at right angles to both lines. Immediately to the north of this road, at the point where it disappeared over the sky-line on the opposite slope, lay the Queen's

Battery House and earthworks, completely commanding the valley on all sides and distant 1,900 yards from our standpoint. Some 1,000 yards down the valley to the north stood a farmhouse, surrounded by a dense plantation, which flanked the valley.

Half-way up the opposite slope, and adjacent to the road, stood an iron house which commanded the drift where the road crossed the above-mentioned watercourse. On the south side of the road, and immediately opposite the last-named iron house, an extensive rectangular stone wall enclosure with high trees formed an excellent advanced central defensive position. Further up the slope, some 500 yards to the south of this enclosure, stretched a line of rifle-pits, which were again flanked to the south by 'prospecting' trenches. On the sky-line numbers of Boers were apparent to our front and right front.

Before reaching the plateau we had observed small parties of Boers hurrying towards Krugersdorp, and immediately on reaching the high ground the rearguard was attacked by the Boer force which had followed the column during the whole morning. I therefore had no further hesitation in opening fire on the Krugersdorp position. The two 7-pounders and the 12½ -pounder opened on the Boer line, making good practice under Captain Kincaid-Smith and Captain Gosling at 1,900 yards. This fire was kept up until 5 p.m. The Boers made practically no reply, but lay quiet in the trenches and battery. Scouts having reported that most of the trenches were evacuated, the first line consisting of the advanced guard (a troop of 100 men), under Colonel White advanced. Two Maxims accompanied this force; a strong troop with a Maxim formed the right and left supports on either flank. Lieutenant-Colonel Grey, with one troop B.B.P. and one Maxim, had been previously detailed to move round and attack the Boers' left. The remaining two troops, with three Maxims, formed the reserve and rearguard.

The first line advance continued unopposed to within 200 yards of the watercourse, when it was checked by an exceedingly heavy cross-fire from all points of the defence. Colonel White then pushed his skirmishers forward into and beyond the watercourse. The left support under Inspector Dykes then advanced to prolong the first line to the left, but, diverging too much to his left this officer experienced a very hot flanking fire from the farmhouse and plantation, and was driven back with some loss. Colonel Grey meanwhile had pushed round on the extreme right and come into action. About this time Major Villiers' patrol returned and reported that the country to our right was open, and that we could easily move round in that direction. It was now evident that the Boers were in great force, and intended holding their position.

Without the arrival of the Johannesburg force in rear of the Boers – an event which I had been momentarily expecting – I did not feel justified in pushing a general attack, which would have certainly entailed heavy losses on my small force. I accordingly left Inspector Drury with one troop and one Maxim to keep in check the Boers who were now lining the edge of the plateau to our left, and placed Colonel Grey with two troops B.B.P., one 12½-pounder, and one Maxim to cover our left flank and continue firing on the battery and trenches south of the road. I then made a general flank movement to the right with the remaining troops.

Colonel Grey succeeded in shelling the Boers out of their advanced position during the next half-hour, and blew up the battery house. Under this cover the column moved off as far as the first houses of the Rand-fontein group of mines, the Boers making no attempt to intercept the movement.

Night was now fast approaching, and still there were no signs of the promised help from Johannesburg. I determined, therefore, to push on with all speed in the direction of that town, trusting in the darkness to slip through any intervening opposition. Two guides were obtained, the column formed in the prescribed night order of march, and we started off along a road leading direct to Johannesburg. At this moment heavy rifle and Maxim fire was suddenly heard from the direction of Krugersdorp, which lay one to one and a half miles to the left rear. We at once concluded that this could only be the arrival of the long-awaited reinforcements, for we knew that Johannesburg had Maxims, and that the Staats-Artillerie were not expected to arrive until the following morning. To leave our supposed friends in the lurch was out of the question. I determined at once to move to their support.

Leaving the carts escorted by one troop on the road I advanced rapidly across the plateau towards Krugersdorp in the direction of the firing, in the formation shown in the accompanying sketch. After advancing thus for nearly a mile the firing ceased, and we perceived the Boers moving in great force to meet the column. The flankers on the right reported another force threatening the flank. Fearing that an attempt would be made to cut us off from the ammunition carts, I ordered a retreat on them. It was now clear that the firing, whatever might have been the cause thereof, was not occasioned by the arrival of any force from Johannesburg. Precious moments had been lost in the attempt to stand by our friends at all costs, under the mistaken supposition that they could not fail to carry out their repeated promises, renewed to us by letter so lately as 11 a.m. this same day. It was now very nearly dark. In the dusk the Boers could be seen closing in on three sides – viz., north, east, and south. The road to Johannesburg appeared completely barred, and the last opportunity of slipping through, which had presented itself an hour ago when the renewed firing was heard, was gone not to return.

Nothing remained but to bivouac in the best position available. But for the unfortunate circumstance of the firing, which we afterwards heard was due to the exultation of the Boers at the arrival of large reinforcements from Potchefstroom, the column would have been by this time (7 p.m.) at least four or five miles further on the road to Johannesburg, with an excellent chance of reaching that town without further opposition.

I moved the column to the edge of a wide vlei to the right of the road, and formed the horses in quarter-column under cover of the slope. The carts were formed up in rear and on both flanks, and five Maxims were placed along the front so as to sweep the plateau. The other three Maxims and the heavy guns were posted on the rear and flank faces. The men were then directed to lie down between the guns and on the side; sentries and cossack posts were posted on each face. Meantime the Boers had occupied the numerous prospecting trenches and cuttings on the plateau at distances from 400 to 800 yards.

At 9 p.m. a heavy fire was opened on the bivouac, and a storm of bullets swept over and around us, apparently directed from all sides except the south-west. The troops were protected by their position on the slope below the level of the plateau, so that the total loss from this fire, which lasted about twenty minutes, was very inconsiderable. The men behaved with admirable coolness, and were as cheery as possible, although very tired and hungry and without water. We were then left unmolested for two or three hours. About midnight another shower of bullets was poured into the camp, but the firing was not kept up for long. Somewhat later a Maxim gun opened on the bivouac, but failed to get our range. At 3.30 a.m. patrols were pushed out on all sides, while the force as silently and rapidly as possible was got ready to move off. At 4 a.m. a heavy fire was opened by the Boers on the column, and the patrols driven in from the north and east sides. Under the direction of Major R. White (assisted by Lieutenant Jesser-Coope) the column was formed under cover of the slope. Soon after this the patrols which had been sent out to the south returned, and reported that the ground was clear of the Boers in that direction. The growing light enabled us to ascertain that the Boers in force were occupying pits to our left and lining the railway embankment for a distance of one and a half miles right across the direct road to Johannesburg. I covered the movements of the main body with the B.B.P. and two Maxims under Colonel Grey along the original left front of the bivouac, and two troops M.M.P., under Major R. White on the right front. During all this time the firing was excessively heavy; however the main body was partially sheltered by the slope.

Colonel White then led the advance for a mile across the vlei without casualty, but on reaching the opposite rise near the Oceanic Mine, was subjected to a very heavy long-range fire. Colonel White hereupon very judiciously threw out one troop to the left to cover the further advance of the main body. This was somewhat delayed, after crossing the rise, by the disappearance of our volunteer guide of the previous night. Some little time elapsed before another guide could be obtained.

In the meantime, Lieutenant-Colonel Grey withdrew his force and the covering Maxims out of action under the protection of the M.M.P. covering troops, and rejoined the main body. At this juncture Colonel Grey was shot in the foot, but most gallantly insisted on carrying on his duties until the close of the action. Sub-Inspector Cazalet was also wounded here, but continued in action until he was shot again in the chest at Doornkop. While crossing the ridge the column was subjected to a very heavy fire, and several men and horses were lost here.

I detailed a rearguard of one troop and two Maxims, under Major R. White, to cover our rear and left flank, and move the remainder of the troops in the ordinary day formation as rapidly forward as possible. In this formation a running rear and flank guard fight was kept up for ten miles.

The 3 maps following, A, B and C were faded and difficult to read. Each was split in two and placed on two opposing pages with over lapping to assist deciphering.
They depict the march and Doornkop.

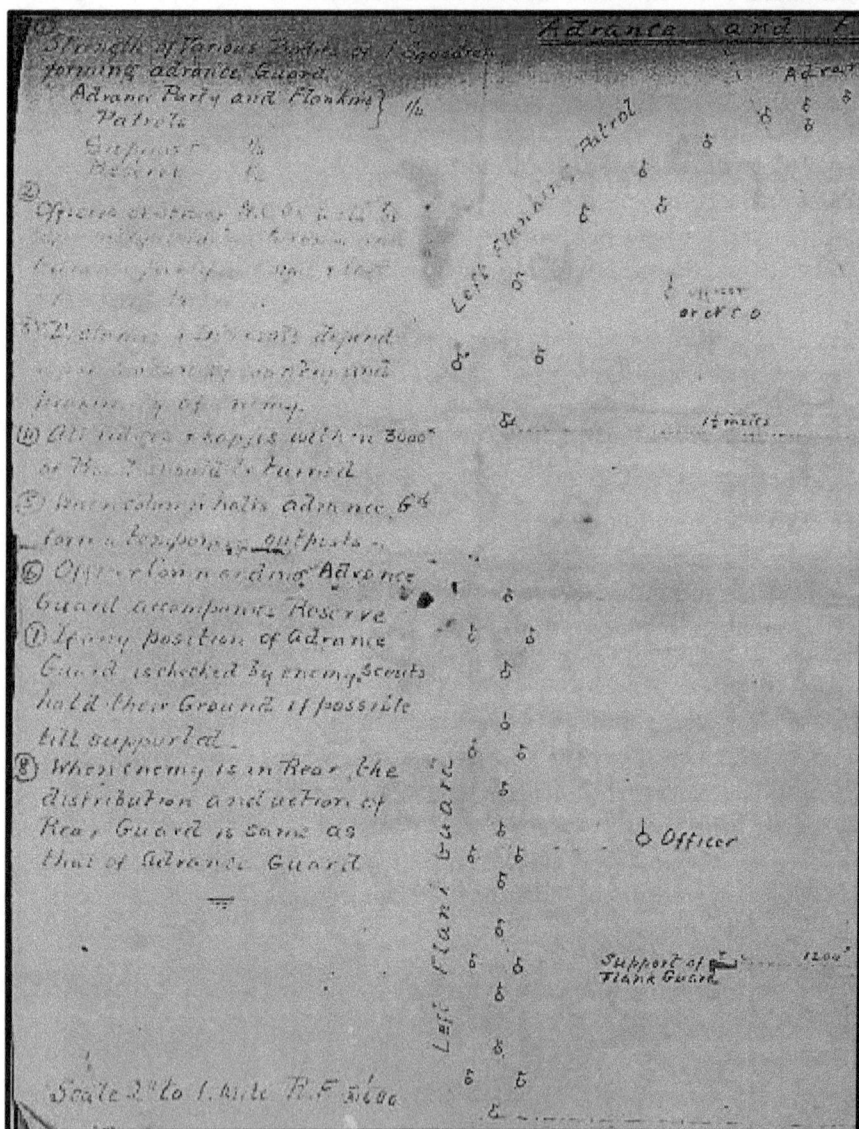

Strength of Various Parties of 1 Squadron
forming advance Guard.
    Advance Party and Flanking } ½
    Patrols
    Support   ¼
    Reserve   ¼

② Officers accompany the Reserve &
the intelligence to Reserve on
Enemy if possible. Reserve &c
do same.

③ Distances of details depend
upon nature of country and
nearness of enemy.

④ All villages + copses within 3000"
on line should be turned.

⑤ Reconnoitering halts advance 6⁴
form a temporary outposts.

⑥ Officer Commanding Advance
Guard accompanies Reserve

⑦ If any position of Advance
Guard is checked by enemy scouts
hold their Ground if possible
till supported.

⑧ When enemy is in Rear, the
distribution and action of
Rear Guard is same as
that of Advance Guard

Scale 2" to 1 Mile B.F 5600

Advance and

Advance

Left Flanking Patrol

office
or O.R.C.O

1½ miles

◊ Officer

Support of
Flank Guard   1200"

Left Flank Guard

Sir John Willoughby's Report   Section Map B

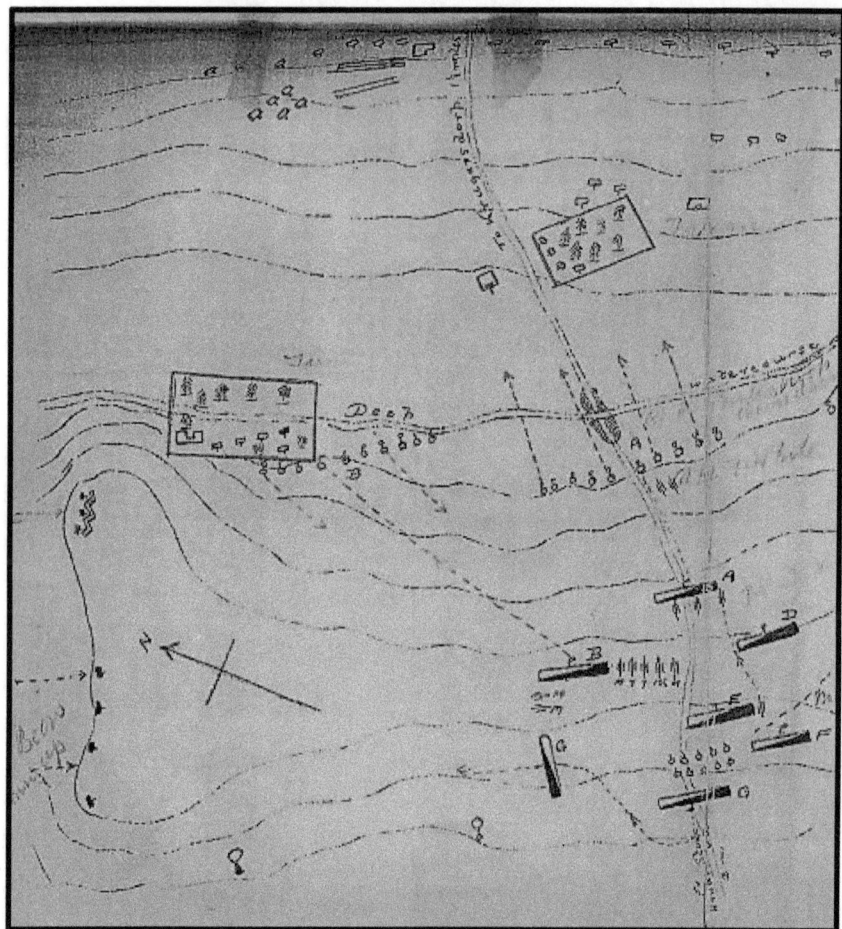

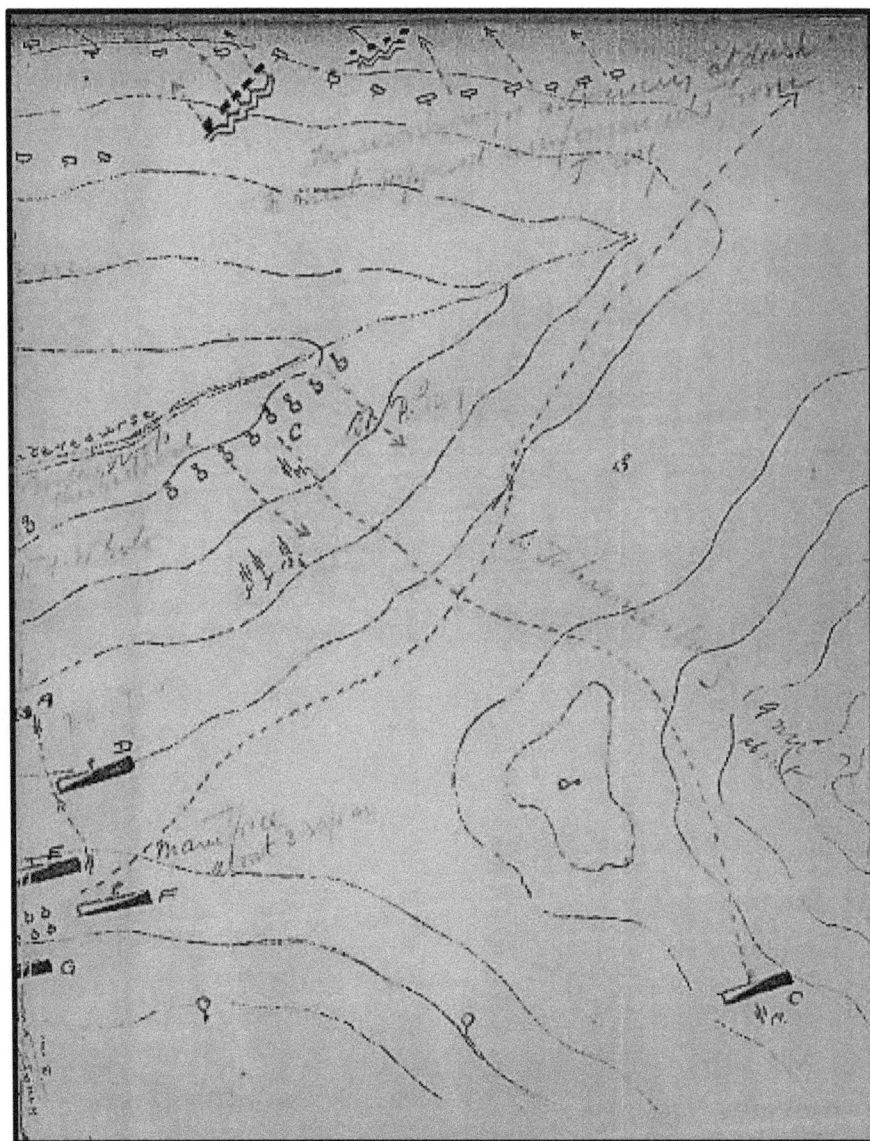

Sir John Willoughby's Report

Section C

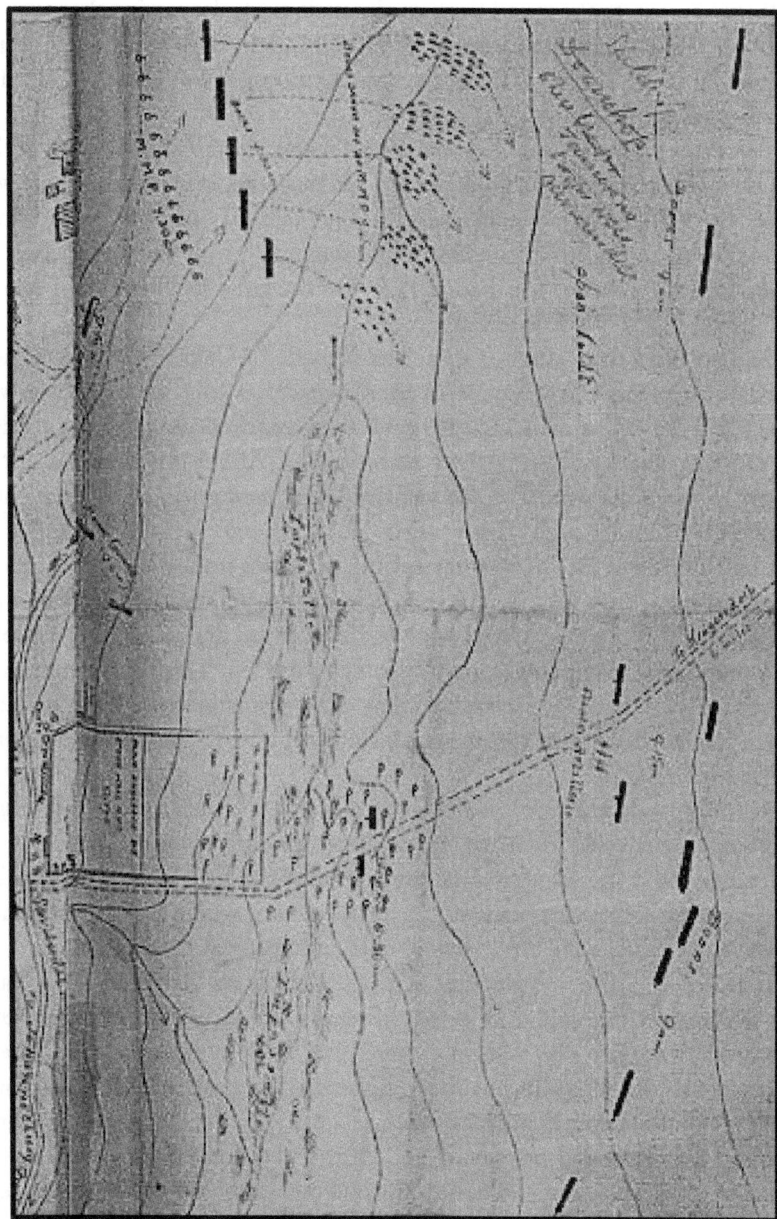

Wherever the features of the ground admitted, a stand was made by various small detachments of the rear and flank guard. In this manner the Boers were successfully kept a distance of 500 yards, and repulsed in all their efforts to reach the rear and flank of the main body. In passing through the various mines and the village of Randfontein we met with hearty expressions of goodwill from the mining population, who professed a desire to help if only they had arms.

Ten miles from the start I received intelligence from Colonel Grey, at the head of the column, that Doornkop, a hill near the Speitfontein mine, was held by 400 Boers, directly barring our line of advance. I repaired immediately to the front, Colonel White remaining with the rear-guard. On arriving at the head of the column, I found the guns shelling a ridge which our guide stated was Doornkop.

The excellent dispositions for the attack made by Colonel Grey were then carried out. The B.B.P., under Major Coventry, who I regret to say was severely wounded and lost several of his men, attacked and cleared the ridge in most gallant style and pushed on beyond it. About this time Inspector Barry received the wound which we have learnt with grief has subsequently proved fatal.

Chief-Inspector Bodle at the same time, with two troops M.M.P., charged, and drove off the field a large force of Boers threatening our left flank. The guide had informed us that the road to the right of the hill was impassable, and that there was open and easy country to the left. This information was misleading. I afterwards ascertained that without storming the Boer position there was no road open to Johannesburg except by a wide detour of many miles to the right.

At this moment Dr. Jameson received a letter from the High Commissioner again ordering us to desist in our advance. Dr. Jameson informed me at the same time of the most disheartening news, viz., that he had received a message stating that Johannesburg would not or could not come to our assistance, and that we must fight our way through unaided.

Thinking that the first ridge now in our hands was Doornkop, we again pushed rapidly on, only to find that in rear of the ridge another steep and stony kopje, some 400 feet in height, was held by hundreds of Boers completely covered from our fire. This kopje effectually flanked the road over which the column must advance at a distance of 400 yards. Scouting showed that there was no way of getting round this hill. Surrounded on all sides by the Boers, men and horses wearied out, outnumbered by at least six to one, our friends having failed to keep their promises to meet us, and my force reduced numerically by one-fourth, I no longer considered that I was justified in sacrificing any more of the lives of the men under me.

As previously explained, our object in coming had been to render assistance, without bloodshed if possible to the inhabitants of Johannesburg. This object would in no way be furthered by a hopeless attempt to cut our way through overwhelming numbers, an attempt, moreover which must without any doubt have entailed heavy and useless slaughter.

With Dr. Jameson's permission, I therefore sent word to the Commandant that we would surrender provided that he would give a guarantee of safe conduct out of the country to every member of the force.

To this Commandant Cronje replied by a guarantee of the lives of all, provided that we would lay down our arms and pay all expenses. In spite of this guarantee of the lives of all, Commandant Malan subsequently repudiated the guarantee in so far as to say that he would not answer for the lives of the leaders, but this was not until our arms had been given up and the force at the mercy of the Boers.

I attribute our failure to reach Johannesburg in a great measure to loss of time from the following causes:

(1) The delay occasioned by the demonstration in front of Krugersdorp, which had been assigned as the place of junction with the Johannesburg force.

(2) The non-arrival of that force at Krugersdorp or of the guides to the Krugersdorp-Johannesburg section of the road, as previously promised by Johannesburg.

(3) The delay consequent on moving to the firing of the supposed Johannesburg column just before dark on Wednesday evening.

I append (1) a sketch-map of the route from Pitsani to Krugersdorp, marked A. This distance (154 miles) was covered in just under 70 hours, the horses having been off-saddled ten times. The 169 miles between Pitsani and Doornkop occupied 86 hours, during 17 of which the men were engaged with the Boers, and were practically without food or water, having had their last meal at 8 a.m. on the morning of the 1st January at Van Oudtshoorn's, 17 miles from Krugersdorp. The average weight carried by each horse was 16 stone.

(2) List of officers engaged in the expedition and composition of the force marked B. From this it will be seen that there was a total of 494 men and officers (exclusive of staff).

(3) Plans of engagements at Krugersdorp and Doornkop, and of the bivouac on the night of January 1st.

I cannot close this narrative without testifying to the very great gallantry and endurance of all officers, non-commissioned officers, and troopers under my command in the field and on the march under most trying circumstances.

COMPOSITION of FORCE

Lt.-Col. Sir John Willoughby, R.H. Guards	Commanding
Major Hon. Robert White, Royal Welsh Fus.	Senior Staff O.
Major C. Hyde-Villiers, Royal Horse Guards	Staff Officer
Captain Kincaid-Smith, Royal Artillery	Artillery S.O.
Captain Kennedy, B.S.A.C.'s Service	Quartermaster
Captain E. Holden, Derbyshire Yeomanry Assistant	Q.M.
Surgeon Captain Farmer, B.S.A. Co.	Medical Officer
Surgeon Captain Seaton Hamilton, late 1st Life Gds	Medical Officer
Lieut. Grenfell, 1st Life Guards	Remount Off.
Lieut. Jesser-Coope, B.S.A. Co.	Transport Off.
Captain Lindsell, late Royal Scots Fusiliers	I/C Scouts
Major J.B. Stracey, Scots Guards)	Officers
Major Heany, B.S.A. Co.)	temporarily
Captain Foley)	attached to
Lieut. Harry R. Holden, late Gren. Gds)	Staff

Officers of Mashonaland Mounted Police

Lt.-Col. Hon. H.F. White, Grenadier Gds	Commanding
Inspector Bodle, late 6th Dragoons	2nd in Command
Inspector Straker Comm.	A Troop
Inspector Dykes Comm.	B Troop
Inspector Barry Comm.	C Troop
Inspector Drury Comm.	D Troop
Sub-Inspectors Scott and Cashel	A Troop
Sub-Inspectors Tomlinson and Chawner	B Troop
Sub-Inspectors Cazalet and Williams	C Troop
Sub-Inspectors Murray and Constable	D Troop
Inspector Bowden and Sub-Inspector Spain	Artillery Troop
Regimental Sergeant-Major Abbott	

Officers of Bechuanaland Border Police

Lt.-Col. Raleigh Grey, 6th Dragoons	Commanding
Major Hon. Charles Coventry	2nd in Command
Captain Gosling Comm.	G Troop
Sub-Lieutenants Hoare and Wood	G Troop
Captain Munroe Comm.	K Troop
Sub-Lieutenant McQueen	K Troop
Surgeon Garraway	Medical Officer
Veterinary Surgeon Lakie	

Numbers:

M.M. Police Officers and men:	372 Pitsani
Staff:	13 Camp
Colony Boys (leading horses, etc.):	65
Horses:	480
Mules:	128

One 12½ -pdr, 6 Maxims, 6 Scotch carts: one Cape Cart, 2 grain waggons.

B.B. Officers and men:	122 Mafeking
Staff:	1 Column
Drivers and leaders:	10
Horses:	160
Mules:	30

Two 7-pdrs, 2 Maxims, 2 Scotch carts, 2 Cape carts.

Totals:

Officers and men:	494
Staff:	14
Drivers, leaders, etc.	75
Horses:	640
Mules:	158
Maxims:	8
12½-pdr:	1
7-pdrs:	229
Scotch Carts:	8
Cape Carts:	3

AMMUNITION

Rounds.

Carried by men and natives:	50,000 Lee-Metford
Carried in Scotch carts and Cape carts:	54,000 Rifle
Total:	104,000
On the Guns:	17,000 Maxim
In carts:	28,000
Total:	45,000
On limber:	44 12½-pdr.
On one Scotch cart:	80
Total:	124
On limbers:	70 7-pdr.
In Scotch carts:	172
Total:	242

The rifle ammunition used was that supplied by the Maxim firm for their guns and also pellet powder. The powder used with the 12½-pounder was was that known as 'ballistite.' Rocket signals and limelights were carried, but not used.

EQUIPMENT CARRIED

On the Person.
(a) Rifle (10 rounds).
(b) Bandolier (60 rounds).
(c) Haversack (1 half-days ration).
(d) Water-bottle filled.

On the Saddle.
(a) Nosebag (5 lb. grain).
(b) Cloak on wallet.
(c) Rifle bucket.
(d) Patrol tin (with grocery ration).
(e) Leather axe-holder (every fourth man)

Near-side wallet, 30 rounds and one half-days rations.
Off-side wallet, 20 rounds, tin dubbin, hold-all, and towel.
Average weight carried by horse was 16 stone. Average weight carried by Scotch carts was 1,600 lb.

The Pitsani Account

This was part of an account found in the B.S.A. Company's books and which was produced in evidence at the trial. The account was obviously set up to handle items of expenditure incurred during and after the raid.

The account is useful as it was used to make payment to members of Jameson's Force that had escaped. This gives confirmation of the existence of the persons named. We do not know if they collected these funds themselves or that the funds were paid to a third party. The money may have been paid to a deceased estate or otherwise, though I feel this would have been unlikely with the short time between the date of the Raid and the date shown. The names that appear on the List who are listed for pay are:

W. Kelsall. A. Chalk. H. Willy. S. Ruck. V.O. Thiebert C. Meyer. W.C. Kelz. J. Manning. C.E. Wiid. R.W. Wilson. F. Dreyer.

Two other names shown were given cash advances to purchase a passage to England. They were:

J.R. Folcher. J.S. Warren.

Could it be possible that these were also members of Jameson's Force that had escaped and they were shown as expenses incurred and charged to this account along with the known escapees on the the 14th January, 1896, twelve days after the surrender at Doornkop.

All these names have been confirmed as escapees. J.H. Wodge was J.H. Dodge, H. Willy was H. Wiley, L.C. Siebert was reported m.i.a., C.E. Wild as d.o.w., E.W. Wen was E.W. Wenn. There is no previous record of a R.W. Wilson, J.R. Folcher or J.S. Warren being part of the Force.

(Two pages of this account are reproduced in the Appendix Section.)

The Daily State

A copy of the Daily State was introduced as part of the evidence at the trial. This document helps to show the gradual build up of the Force during the month of December, 1895.

(A page is reproduced in the Appendix Section, divided in two for clarity. The notes in the margin are the source of new names.)

The names mentioned are:

Dec. Date:	Name:	Note
2	Inspector Dykes	Arrived with B Troop
3	Sub-Insp. Bowden	Arrived with Artillery Troop
4	S/Major Spain	Promoted Sub-Inspector
	Tpr. Constable	Arrived in camp
	Tpr. Carpenter	Arrived in camp
5	No. 559 Tpr. G.	Long Attested
6	Inspector Southey	Arrived with C Troop
7	Sgt. Cazalet	Promoted Sub-Inspector
	Tpr. W.G. Murray	Promoted Sub-Inspector
8	Cpl. S. Ruck	Promoted Sgt.
	Tpr. Lester	Promoted Sgt-Major
	Mr. Cashel Arrived.	Apptd. Sub-Inspector
9	Tpr. J. Newman	Taken on
	No. 1790 Cpl. Tapp	Promoted 3rd Class Sgt.
	Cpl. Stapleton	Promoted 3rd Class Sgt.
11	Mr. 'No Name'	Arrived. Apptd. Inspector
	Sgt. Malone	Reduced
	L. Gorringe	Attested
	W. Pescod	Attested
12	J. Armstrong	Attested
16	L. Tolling	Attested
	Tpr. Rademeyer	Discharged
18	Kerr	Struck Off – Deserted
	Woodcock	Struck Off – Deserted
	B. Gunn	Attested
20	Hillier	Discharged
24	S. Clarendon	Attested
	Stanley	Struck Off
	Farr/Major Masters	Promoted Sub.-Inspector
28	Tpr. Brent	Discharged

Force Strength

The numbers that were involved in the Raid from various sources, including escapees and casualties.

Source	Total	Detail
Marshall-Hole	510	Quoting source as *Story of an African Crisis* by Garrett and Edwards, 1898
Colin Harding	511	*Frontier Patrols* 1936
Lt.-Col. Bodle	504	Possibly does not include the six non-Combatants
Gaberone Archives	510	Could number 511 with addition of Tpr. Townsend
Volksrust Roll	463	Volksrust, including six non-combatants and twenty at Pretoria in hospital
	3	Bleulah who deserted plus McCarthy and Power detained at Pretoria
	23	Known and possible escapees
Total	513	
Missing or escaped	17	Escapees confirmed by documentary evidence.

As previously stated this will never be a complete and accurate list, as it is inevitable that names missed will come to light from time to time. Some of these will have taken part, others will have given themselves the credit for participation for their own reasons. We can only include what has been substantiated.

Other names that have been mentioned in the Gaberone Archives but do not appear elsewhere but (sic) have been included in the list are Campbell and Townsend. The Pitsani Account extract gives some names that could have been connected with the raid. It must be remembered that there would have been indecision on the part of many, some could have joined at the last moment, others could have changed their minds and decided not to proceed.

The African and Coloured members of the Force were said to have numbered seventy-five, forty-one appear on the Volksrust list. I assume the remainder escaped and merged with the local populace and workers.

It is impossible to reconcile the numbers given by the various sources so I leave readers to make their own calculations if these numbers are considered important.

White's Diary

Following is an extract from Major White's diary, the diary that figured so prominently in the trial. It was captured by the Boers and passed through the hands of the British Authorities, then after the trial it was handed to the South African Government who returned the diary to White in the early 1900s. When he died he bequeathed his papers to the Rhodes House Library at Oxford where the diary now rests.

These are some of the entries to do with recruitment, the names in bold type appear on the roll.

Nov Date Entries

8   At Mafeking enrolled the following men for police: **Hanly, Clements, Haddingham, Gibbs, Thomas, Jackson, Mein**. No discharge papers, 19th Hussars, one month's probation, O'Connell. One month's probation, W. Raadt, **H. Place**. Herbert Bleider, one month's probation.

9   Advances £1 to **Jardine**, police.

10   Enrolled **Lewis, Moras, Nickson, Jack, Morris** and Owen.

11   Enrolled Aleck, Stevens, **Jones, John Gall.**

15   Engaged following: Salaman, **Brown, Don Newman, Phillbrick, Major, Keenan**, Stanley Correspondent, Guard, one month's probation, 5th and 12th Lancers no discharge papers. Also **Getcliffe, Martin, Gray, Champken**, Valence.

18   Paid Bradley £6.6s and discharged him.

19   **Vanner, C. Kennedy, Ryan, Hayes**, Fanhurst, **Gooch, Brooks, Mackenzie** (Scots Greys one month's probation), **Marchant, Shaw, Oliver, Bryan, Meyers, Flynn**, Byrne, **Poole** (one month's probation), **Macnamara, P. Moroney** (one month's probation) enrolled.

20   Jacobs, B.B.P. deserted, also wanted as deserter from C.M.R., **Spurrier** (late R.H.A. and Trojan) also telegraph work, **Hillary** (B.B.P.), **Sainsbury, Adams** (recommended by Major Panzera), **Wud** (Garrant at Cape Town), **Therebert, Delahaye** (Medical Staff Corps), Henny, 8 years DEOHR, sergeant, **Stevenson** 18 month's DEOHR, sergeant, **Wedderburn** (8 years 3rd Batt. North. Frs.) **Holt** (3 years DEOHR), **McMillan** (4 years DEOHR), **Hennesay** (10 years at sea), **T. Gordon** (9 years at sea), **Kelsall** (one

month's probation, 5 years Y. & L., no discharge papers),
Rankine (19th Hussars), **O'Farrell**. Newman, tenderfoot,
left.

Names in bold type possibly on main roll of prisoners.

Spurious Claimants to fame.

As is inevitable with events of this importance there are persons who wish
to participate in the limelight. I have come across a few suspects which fit
this category. This seems to occur in Medal sale catalogues where the
Jameson Raider in the description may have been inserted to increase the
value of the lot.

The most prominent of these people was the claim of Captain Thatcher
which reached the pages of *The Times* of the day.

(*See Appendix for reproduction of a letter refuting his claim*).

The prisoners waiting at Volksrust railway goods yard

The first trainload of prisoners leaving Charlestown en-route to Durban

Dr. Jameson and others leaving Pretoria Gaol

En-route to England aboard the *Victoria*
Back row: Kincaid-Smith. H.F. White. Jameson. Villiers.
R. White. Stacey. Grey.
Front row: Coventry. Willoughby. Lindsell. Grenfell.

Telegraphic report of Sir Hercules Robinson (Pretoria) to Mr. Chamberlain

(Received 10.15 p.m., 11th January, 1896. TNA Ref. CO 879/44. No. 150)

11th January – No. 4. Following is list of casualties in Jameson's Force as far as can be ascertained. In many cases initials cannot be obtained as rolls were lost.

Killed:
A Troop: 120 Sergeant Ruck, Troopers 452 N. Black, 313 Sheppard.
B Troop: Troopers 343 Bletsoe, 488 Edwards, 368 Hutchinson.
C Troop: Corporals 275 Beard, 426 Maree, Trooper 202 J. Myer.
D Troop: Troopers 547 Hennessey, 549 Forster.
Artillery Troop: Trooper 324 Still.
G. Troop: late B.B.P. Troopers J.B. Lamb and Reelands.
K. Troop: late B.P.P. Troopers 1155 D.B. Stone and F. Osler.

Wounded Dangerously:
Inspector William John Barry of Ballyvonare, Cork. Troopers David Fraser (son of General Sir David Fraser). Paul Wiid of Cape Town.

Severely: Francis Mostyn, 10 Spencer Hill, Wimbledon. Stewart Bruce of Cardean Street, Dundee. Corporal Frederick Dreyer of Portnolloth. Francis Nickson, Park Hill, Towcester. Ernest Barnes, care of Mrs Godfrey Merton, Surrey. James Mevity, Oldham Road, Manchester. William McLachlan, care of F. Richardson, 28 Fenchurch Street. Sampson Burrowes, Holden Brewery, Birmingham. Dermir Fyvie of Natal. Thomas Lynn, Leighton Terrace, Galashiels.

Following slightly wounded or in hospital from sickness – all doing well:
Colonel Gray, Major Crosse, Captain Coventry, Sub-Inspector Cazalet.
A Troop: Troopers 492 F.W. Brown, 494 Phillbrick, 279 George Potter, 482 H.C. Gibbs, Malcolm Den and Granville Pomeroy.
D Troop: Trooper 569 L. Gorringe.
G Troop: Troopers George Payne, Arthur Rowley, Frederick Stannard of 134 Kennington Park Road, Frederick Hayes of Marlborough, Wiltshire, E.A. Berry, T.M. Brooke, Edward Furmery, Henry Callanan, Alfred Walters, Alexander Gardner, Charles Hoskins, Gwynne Harwood, James Burnand, Cecil Rowe, William Law, Thomas Willows, Richard Brown,

Harry Steer, William Mack, Harold Adams, Acton, Arthur Pail, Henry Shone, Cecil Maloney, Frederick Walker. Troop not known John Wilson of 33 Oval, Hackney, Musgrave Beardon late C.M.R.

Missing:

A Troop: Troopers 414 Valle, 77 Weinthal.

B Troop: Troopers 477 Haddington, 362 Kirkpatrick, 402 Williams, 413 Wiley, 206 Larson, Dodge (number unknown).

C Troop: Troopers 556 Coghill, 527 Kelsall, 439 Pattinson, 352 Siebert, 524 Thiebert.

D Troop: 254 Corporal Kebz, 250 T. Willan, 553 Holt, 550 Edgecombe, 166 Manning.

G Troop: 1351 Corporal Ballard.

K Troop: Farr, Corporal Davidson, 2286 Trooper Chalke, 1650 Friedman, 2169 Hall, 2256 Logan.

Many of these are supposed to have escaped to Johannesburg. I sent one of my staff to visit the wounded in Krugersdorp yesterday and he reports that the hospital is clean and comfortable and the men well looked after. Inform Lord Coventry his son is getting on wonderfully well, the wound being only slight. He was cheerful and happy and said he wanted nothing but a little money, which has been supplied. Regret to state that I have just heard that Trooper David Fraser died this morning of his wounds.

Contemporary Accounts of the Raid

Apart from the account written by Willoughby for the War Office there are numerous personal accounts of the Raid that help to show a more personal approach to the venture than the standard texts.

Diary of Col. J. Stracey. Clitherow: Diary and letters of Trooper Leonard Gorringe: Diary and papers of Trooper Edward Leary; and the account by Col. A.J. Tomlinson, later Acting Commissioner of the B.S.A.P.

1. National Archives, Kew. CO/179/193
2. National Archives, Kew. WO/32/7839
3. National Archives, Kew. BT/26/89
4. National Archives, Kew. WO 32/7839
5. National Archives, Kew. WO 32/7839
6. National Archives, Kew. DPP/1/2/1 to 4
7. National Army Museum. (Clitherow) 6603/52 [ref 2024: 1966-03-52]
8. National Army Museum. (Gorringe) 8218/19 [ref 2024: 1982-12-19]
9. National Army Museum. (Leary) APFS 1999-07-21 [ref 2024: 1999-07-20]
10. *The Outpost* Author's possession. (Tomlinson)

APPENDICES

Reproduction of page of *The Critic*   47
Reproduction of Pitsani Camp Account   48/49
Reproduction of *Daily State*   50/51
Reproduction of Thatcher Letter to *The Times*   52
The Sentences   52
Letter on Disposal of Personnel   53
List of Witnesses   54
Rifles   54

Note: Copy of the article is illegible in the original edition

PITSANI CAMP ACCOUNT IN THE B. S. A. Co.'s BOOKS.

1896.			£ s. d.	£ s. d.
Jan.	14	To C. J. Holt, pay, 1 to 28 Dec., @ 7/6 per day ..	10 10 0	
		,, W. Kelsall, pay, 1 to 28 Dec., @ 7/6 per day ..	10 10 0	
		,, A. Chalk, pay, 16 to 28 Dec.	4 17 6	
		,, J. H. Wodge, pay, 1 to 28 Dec.	10 10 0	
		,, H. Willy, pay, 1 to 28 Dec.	10 10 0	
		,, S. Ruck, pay, 1 to 28 Dec., @ 9/- per day	12 12 0	
		,, W. Kelsall, pay, 16 to 28 Dec., @ 3/- per day, as Regtl. tailor	1 19 0	
		,, L. Valle, pay, 1 to 28 Dec., @ 7/6 per day.. ..	10 10 0	
		,, V. O. Thiebert, pay, 1 to 28 Dec., @ 7/6 per day	10 10 0	
		,, O. Meyer, pay, 1 to 28 Dec., @ 7/6 per day ..	10 10 0	
		,, W. J. Kirkpatrick, pay, 1 to 28 Dec., @ 7/6 p.day	10 10 0	
		,, W. C. Kelz, pay, 1 to 28 Dec., @ 8/- per day ..	11 4 0	
		,, J. Manning, pay, 1 to 28 Dec., @ 7/6 per day ..	10 10 0	
		,, L. C. Siebert, pay, 1 to 28 Dec., @ 7/6 per day ..	10 10 0	
	18	,, R. Levino, bootmaker ..	8 15 6	
		,, Mosenthal & Co., P.E. ..	16,077 8 6	
		,, T. W. Beckett & Co., clothing	46 19 0	
	27	,, Carr. on Luggage ..	16 5 4	
		,, Stand. Bank, dishonoured cheques, o/a W. Bodle	14 12 6	
	28	,, Postages on parcels, Jameson's column	4 2 3	
		,, C. K. Wild, pay, 1 to 28 Dec., at 7/6 per day ..	10 10 0	
		,, R. W. Wilson, pay, 1 Dec. to 12 Jan., @ 7/6 p.day	14 2 6	
	29	,, Postages on parcels	5 10 8	
		,, T. guard, 3 mos. to 31 Jan.	23 5 0	

Expanded image of 'Remarks' Column of page 50

PITSANI CAMP ACCOUNT—*Continued.*

1896.			£	s.	d.	£	s.	d.
Jan.	29	To Exch. on credit, £16,077 8s. 6d.	20	4	6			
		,, Salisbury office	275	2	11			
Feb.	1	,, Baggage, S.O. 706 and 707	4	13	6			
		,, Railage on Tprs.' luggage	3	5	7			
		,, ,, ,,	2	5	11			
		,, Julius Weil	106	15	0			
		,, Telegrams in January ..	26	14	0			
		By 2 horses taken over by Telegraph Department	..			50	0	0
		To coolie hire re baggage ..	2	11	9			
		,, Freight on luggage to England	167	19	5			
		,, 100 labels	0	4	0			
	7	,, Postages on tprs.' letters to London	5	12	6			
	10	,, Wages, Manning and Thiebert	3	0	0			
		,, 3rd class passage, Spiers, to Durban	4	10	0			
		,, Cash, do.	2	10	0			
		,, ,, Hon. C. J. Coventry	100	0	0			
		,, Postages on tprs.' letters to London	0	18	4			
		,, Stand. Bk., W. Bodle's chq.	35	5	6			
	17	,, ,, ,, ,,	45	2	0			
		,, ,, ,, ,,	47	1	0			
		By Major Forbes				1,733	6	5
		To James Laurence & Co. ..	43	12	6			
		,, ,, ,,	18	11	10			
		,, Cheque, Insp. W. Bodle..	9	15	0			
		By Entry reversed	..			16,077	8	6
		To Freight on luggage to England	105	13	10			
		,, J. H. Folcher, cash o/s passage to England ..	20	0	0			
		,, W. Wen, pay, 1 to 28 Dec.	10	10	0			
		,, W. Bodle's chq., Stand. Bk.	10	4	6			
	27	,, F. Dreyer, pay, 1 to 28 Dec.	11	18	0			
		,, W. Bodle's cheque, favour Sedgwick & Co. ..	20	5	0			
		,, Major Forbes' expenses to Maf.	30	15	0			
	28	,, K. S. Warren, on account passage money to England	12	0	0			

Attached			Remarks
Officer	ncos	men	

(The Remarks column contains handwritten entries, largely illegible:)

Insp. Hughes & B. Tp and 3 Off. 3 ncos 64 men & 76 horses

Sub Insp. Broden with artillery and 1 Off. 1 nco 32 men 43 horses

Sgt. maj. Spain promd. Sub Insp. Tpr. Constable with Tpr. Carpenter arrived 57 horses taken over no. 557 Tpr. Lg. Long attested

Insp. Lindsay with "C" Tp and 3 Off. 10 Sgts 3 ncos 8 cs 58 men 76 horses

5 men attested to date 2nd 7 horses taken on strength Sgt. Onglet & Tpr. W.G. Murray from [illegible] Corpl. L. Smith from Tp. Tpr. Salon from 2m. [illegible] Casket and 1 applied Sub Insp.

J. Newman taken on to date 25/11/95 - 62 horses taken over from M.O.P. 3 men taken on to date 6.12.95 1 horse taken on number 1760 Corpl. Insp. Hampden promoted 3rd Cl.

Mr. [illegible] arrived Supft. Insp. Lg. Malone relieve 6 horses taken on - Insp. Lindsay proceeds to [illegible] L. Gorringe mr. passed attested to date 9.12.95

J. Armstrong attested

Horse no. 782 shot for glanders

52 Remounts taken over

1 Remount taken over

L. Tolling attested - Tpr. Rademeyer discharged 1 remount taken on

3 remounts taken on - Horse 668 struck off. 13 have 1 Woodcock struck off as deserters Guinn attested - 32 remounts taken on

Millin dischgd.

6 horses transft to M.O.P. 1 man attested Insp. Drury arid from leave. 1 Remount no. 573 taken on 2 men attested. Horse 653 dead

L. Clarendon attested - Stanley struck off. Secr. major Masters from Sub. Insp.

Tpr. Brett discharged

THE SENTENCES

On the arrival of the officers of the raiding party in England, Dr. Jameson was smuggled up the Thames in the police steamer, and landed at Waterloo Bridge, hereby avoiding the demonstration that would have ensued on his recognition by the populace. But he and his comrades received a most enthusiastic greeting in Bow Street, and at the Court next day, when they were charged under the Foreign Enlistment Act. On July 20th, they were brought to the bar for trial before Lord Chief Justice Russell, Baron Pollock, and Mr. Justice Hawkins. There they were found guilty, as Lord Russell had

DR. JAMESON'S TROOPERS AND CAPTAIN THATCHER.

TO THE EDITOR OF THE TIMES.

Sir,—On our arrival at Las Palmas *en route* for England we were vastly surprised to find various accounts of Dr. Jameson's march, fights, &c., contributed to your columns, and to those of other papers, by an individual describing himself as Captain Thatcher.

These statements published in a less influential organ than *The Times* would not be worth refuting, but as the case stands the public should not be misled further by this man's pretensions and utterly unreliable statements.

He was recognized by one of our officers at Malmani, on the line of march, as an ex-corporal of the 17th Lancers, who succeeded in obtaining a commission, but for some reason or other left the service shortly after.

Some 50 miles from our starting point he galloped after and caught us up, apparently in a fright, stating that Boers were in rear of us, which was perfectly untrue. Here he was allowed to remain with the column, as he begged hard for that privilege, but was suspected of being a spy and treated as such. He rode with the column until we reached Krugersdorp, after which he disappeared. His statements that he was in charge of a Maxim gun ; that he was galloper to Dr. Jameson ; that he offered to hold the Boers in check with 500 Johannesburgers ; that the column was composed of lads from public schools, &c., are fabrications, and as ridiculous as they are untrue.

Our apology for asking you to give publicity to this must be our desire to expose an impostor.

We are, Sir, yours faithfully,
W. BODLE, Chief Inspector Police.
LAWSON L. B. DYKES,
FRANK L. BOWDEN, } Inspectors.
M. STRAKER,
G. V. DRURY,
Matabeleland Mounted Police.

directed in a strong and comprehensive speech, but the jury accompanied their finding with a rider that the state of things in Johannesburg presented great provocation. Dr. Jameson was sentenced to fifteen months imprisonment, Sir John Willoughby to ten, Major Robert White to seven, Colonel Henry White and Major Coventry to five, all without hard labour. The last however, who was suffering from the severe wound he had received at Doornkop, was released almost at once and the Doctor, whose health had been gravely endangered in prison, was released early in December. The men had previously been allowed to return to their homes by the President of the Transvaal.

Correspondence on disposal of personnel.
Confirmation of take-over of control of the B.S.A Company's Police.

66

I cannot do better than send you copy further correspondence I have had with the solicitor. You will notice that 11 only of the Company's servants are required in connexion with the proceedings against Dr. Jameson and others, and that the remainder of the men need not longer be detained in this country.

I understand that you have already made arrangements for sending away the men not detained, and it only occurs to me to add that, as I understand the Company's police force has not been disbanded, but that its control will be taken over by Colonel Sir R. E. Martin, K.C.M.G., who is to be the Commandant-General of the Company's forces, it seems to follow that the men and their officers not now under arrest should return to their duties. I gather they still continue in the Company's pay, and that, since their arrival in England, they have received the January and February pay.

With reference to the Colonial Office letter of the 11th instant, transmitting a list of persons who arrived in the "Harlech Castle," and who reside out of this country, I think you should point out that these persons are included among those of the Company's forces who have received pay as above-mentioned, and that, in these circumstances, it is scarcely reasonable that in addition they should have an allowance for maintenance. Perhaps, however, the point is not very material, for I am informed that two of the men, Carson and Moras, have already been sent away, and that the others, except Bernstein, will shortly leave.

Bernstein, you will notice, is included in the list sent by the solicitor to the Treasury in his letter of the 14th instant. I imagine that the Treasury will take over the maintenance of the men included in that list, and that their pay should, therefore, cease after a date to be agreed upon—say, perhaps, the 31st instant, if, as I believe, payment is monthly, and made on the last day of each month.

Believe me, &c.
BOURCHIER F. HAWKSLEY.

The Secretary,
British South Africa Company.

Correspondence on List of witnesses required for the Jameson Trial.

DEAR SIR,   Treasury, Whitehall, S.W., March 14, 1896.
     WITH reference to your former correspondence, I beg to inform you that, so far
as the prosecution are concerned, they have no desire that any of the men in the service
of the Chartered Company should be detained longer in this country, with the exception
of those who have already been subpœnaed, and a list of whose names I enclose.

I have forwarded to the Colonial Office a copy of this letter.

                                                      Faithfully yours,
     B. F. Hawksley, Esq., Solicitor,   .   H. CUFFE.
          Mincing Lane, E.C.

LIST of PERSONS in the Service of the BRITISH SOUTH AFRICA COMPANY who have
     been subpœaned as WITNESSES for the Prosecution in the case REGINA v. JAMESON
     and OTHERS.

                    Chief Inspector Bodle.
                    Trooper Charles Henry Kitson.
                    Lance-Corporal W. H. Smith.
                    Trooper Philip L. Hill.
                    Sergeant A. B. Cumming.
                    Sergeant Sidney Charles Ruck.
                    Trooper William Beale.
                    Trooper R. N. Burnside.
                    Captain Gerald Ellis.
                    Trooper A. E. Walters.
                    Armourer H. L. Bernstein.

Extract from "The Lee-Enfield Story" by Ian Skennerton published by Greenhill Books.

Page 67.

The British South Africa Co. purchased a few thousand Mk I* and Mk II Lee-Metford
rifles between December 1894 and September 1895, along with 380 Lee-Metford
sporting models with a flat rib along the top of the barrel. These too were "Volunteer
patterns" or commercial production without the Government markings (Royal cypher
and year of manufacture along with the military mark designation) on the butt socket:
only the patent acknowledgement and manufacturer were marked at this position. Many
of these rifles were purchased in haste for rapid consignment to South Africa and on
one occasion the B.S.A.factory worked all night to complete such rifles for shipment the
next morning.

Many of these rifles were used in the Jameson Raid, as hundreds of rifles were seized
and later observed in Pretoria to have the B.S.A & M Co. markings.

The prices quoted for these products at the time were:-

Lee-Metford Sporting Rifle.	£6/10/-
Lee-Metford Mk I*.	£4/-/-
Lee-Metford Mk II.	£5/-/-

JAMESON RAID 1895 – 96 NOMINAL ROLL/SERVICE RECORDS

No.	Name/Prev. Mil. Service	Rank	Post	Dom.	Address/remarks	Disp.
1	Jameson, Sir Leander S.	Leader		Scot.	Late PM Cape Colony Died 16.11.17	Vic
2	Willoughby, Sir John C. Bart. Major, R.H. Gds	Cmmdt	Staff	Eng.	Oxfordshire Egypt 1885. BSACP 1890 & 1893. Died 16.4.18	Vic
3	White, Hon. Henry F. Major, Gren. Gds	Col.	Staff	Eng.	Commissioner BSAP	Vic
4	Grey, Raleigh 1881-89, Capt. 6th Innis'n Drgns 1889-95 BBP	Col.	Staff	Eng.	1899-1902 Rhod. Field F. CMG 1896 CVO 1910 KBE 1919	Vic
5	White, Hon. Robert Capt. Royal Welsh Fus.	Major	Staff	Eng.	Brig. Gen. CB, CMG, DSO	Vic
6	Stracey, John Bourchier Major, Scots Gds	Major	Staff NAM Papers Ref. 6603/52	Eng.	Family name change; Lt.Col. JS Clitheroe, CBE	Vic
7	Villiers, Charles Hyde Capt. Royal H. Gds	Major	Staff	Eng.	Grosvenor Sq. London 1899-1902 CO SA Light H.	Vic
8	Coventry, Hon. Charles J. Capt. 3rd Worcs.Reg. 1893 Capt. BBP 1895-96	Major	Staff	Eng.	Major BSAP Colonel, CB	Vic
9	Cross, Charles W. Major 5th Iniskilling Drs.	Major			Non-combatant, parolled to Cape Town	
10	Heany, Maurice David 1890, Capt. Pioneers 1893 Capt. Salisbury H.	Major	Staff	USA	Bulawayo, Matabeleland Died Bulawayo 26.6.27	Vic
11	Kincaid-Smith, Kenneth J. Lieut. RA	Capt.	Staff	Eng.	Ashdean,Chichester. Col. 1899-1902 SA War DSO. 1905-07 WAFF. WWI CMG 1916, CB 1919	Vic
12	Monro, Charles Lloyd D. Capt. 3rd Batt. Seaforth H. 1893 Lieut. BBP	Capt.	K	Scot.	Allen Freres, Rosshire 1897-1902 Capt. BSAP	Vic
13	Foley, Cyril P. Capt. 3rd Batt. Royal Scots	Capt.	Staff	Scot.	24, Bolton St. London	Vic

14	Holden, Edward C.S. Capt. Derbyshire Yeo.	Capt.	Staff	Scot.	Aston, Derbyshire	Vic
15	Lindsell, Charles Fred. Capt. 4th Batt. Durham L.I. & R. Scots Fus.	Capt.	Staff	Scot.	c/o 41 WLJ, Newcastle on Tyne. 1899-02 Sgt. 452 E. Sqn Rhod. Regiment	Vic
16	Gosling, Audley Vaughan 1877-79 S. Africa	Capt.	Staff	Bech.	c/o Isthmian Club, London 1896-1903 Major, Rifle Bgde attached BSAP	HC
17	Holden, Harry R.L. Lieut. Grenadier Gds	Capt.	Staff 35	Eng.	Guards Club, Pall Mall, London	HC
18	Grenfell, Harold M. Lieut. 1st Life Gds	Lieut.	Staff	Eng.	69, Eaton Place, London S.W.	Vic
19	Kennedy, James H. 1893 Capt. Salisbury H.	Capt/ QM	Staff 43	Ire.	Salisbury,Mashonaland	HC
20	Jesser-Coope, John C. 1890 Tpr. BSACP	Lieut.	Staff 27	Eng.	Bulawayo, Matabeleland 1896 Capt. MRF. 1899/02 Capt. SRV. WWI 2nd Rhod. Reg. Died 29.6.50	HC
21	Hore, Arthur Henry J. 1893 S/M 1299 BBP	Sub.Lt	G 36	Eng.	40, St Stevens Ave, Ldn W. 1896 Lieut. MRF. 1898 Mash. Const. 1899-1902 Capt. SRV. Died -.8.1941	HC
22	McQueen, William James	Sub.Lt	G 32	Eng.	3, Woodchurch Rd. W. Ham- stead, Lon. 1896 Lieut. MRF. 1897-1902 Capt. BSAP	HC
23	Wood, Edward Allan 2nd Drgns & 17th Lanc.	Sub.Lt	K 27	Eng.	'Ascot' Gordon Rd. Ealing, London. 1914-18 Brig. Gen. DSO 2 Bars, CMG, C de G R.I.C. Died 20.5.30. SeeWWH	HC
24	Bodle, William BBP. BSACP. Salisbury H. 1893	Ch/Insp	Staff 42	Eng.	Bulawayo, Matabeleland 1896 Major MRF & BSAP 1899-02 Lt.Col. CMG. Comm. BSAP. Brig. Gen. 1914-18 Died 1924.	HC

25	Straker, Martin 1893 Sgt. Victoria Col.	Insp.	A 36	Eng.	Bulawayo, Matabeleland Capt. MRF 1899-02 Major BSAP.1902 Coronation	HC
26	Dykes, Lawson Leigh B. 1890 Pioneers. 1893 Sby.H	Insp.	B 30	Eng.	Bulawayo, Matabeleland 1896 Insp. Town Police	HC
27	Drury, Gordon Vallancy 1893 Lieut. BBP	Insp.	D 28	Eng.	Bulawayo, Matabeleland 1896 Capt. MRF. 1899-02 Capt. BSAP.	HC
28	Bowden, Frank Lake 1893 Cpl. Vic. Col. 1894 MMP No. 70	Insp.	Art. 29	Eng.	Bulawayo, Matabeleland 1896 Capt. MRF. 1899-02 Capt. BSAP. DSO. Died in Service 26.6.1906	HC
495	Barry, William John H. 1890, No. 159 Pioneers 1893 Capt. BBP. 5th Batt. Munster Fusiliers.	Insp.	C	Ire.	Butlerant Ballyvonare, Cork, Ireland. 1894 MMP No. 170 Died & buried Krugersdorp 1.2.1896	---
29	Scott, Harry Farquhar MMP No. 220	S.Insp.	A 20	Eng.	7, Grosvenor Gdns London	HC
30	Cashell, Rowan Capt. Retired.	S.Insp.	A	C.C.	Cape Town 1896 Lt. MRF. Capt.SRV 1899-02. Died -.9.1926	RC
31	Musters, Henry Arthur C.	S. Insp.	A 27	Eng.	Bulawayo, Matabeleland 1896 Capt. MRF. Vet. Officer	HC
32	Chawner, Henry William 1893 Lieut. Raaf's Col. MMP No. 1.	Sub.Insp	B	Mat.	Bulawayo, Matabeleland 1896 Lt. Gwelo Vol. 1899-09 Capt. BSAP. D.9/41	RC
33	Tomlinson, Alfred James 1894 MMP	Sub.Insp.	B 25	Eng.	11 Marine Sq. Brighton Eng. 1896 Lt. MRF; 1899-02 Lt. BSAP. 1914-18 Lt.Col. Act. Comm. BSAP. D. 1961	HC
34	Murray, Walter Pringle E.	Sub.Insp.	C 23	Scot.	40, Montgomery Rd, Kelvinside, Glasgow 1896 Lt. MRF, 99-02 Lt BSAP	HC
35	Williams,Gresham Hugh P. 1890, Sgt. BSACP	Sub.Insp.	C 25	Eng.	Manor Ho.,Skelton, York 1896 Lt. MRF. 1899-02 Capt. BSAP. Later 21st Lanc.	HC

58

No.	Name / Details	Rank		Nat.	Location / Notes	
36	Cazalet, Alexander Phillip.L.Sub.Insp. 1893 Cpl. 1994 BBP MMP No. 133		D 34	Eng.	Bulawayo, Matabeleland 1896 Lt. MRF. 1899-02 Capt. BSAP	HC
37	Constable, Harry Paley 1890 Tpr. 737 BSACP 1893 Sby. H. '94 MMP 108	Sub.Insp.	D 26	Eng.	Clifton, Bristol 1895 Lt. MRF Died Port Elizabeth 11.6.01	HC
38	Spain, Walter Smithey 1893 Tpr. BBP 1653 MMP No. 99	Sub.Insp.	Art. 23	Eng.	10, Victoria Sq. Newcastle on Tyne.1899-18 Major BSAP HC 1918 Mjr KRRC?. D. 26.12.39	
39	Hamilton, Seaton G. Surg. Capt. 1st Life Gds	Surg/Lt.	Staff 43	Eng.	Naval & Military Club, Piccadilly, London	HC
40	Farmer, William H.F.	Surg/Lt.	Staff 32	Eng.	24, Upper Wimpole St. London, WI	HC
41	Garraway, Edward C.F. 1893 Surg/Lt BBP	Surg/Lt	K 32	Ire.	Rookshire, Waterford, Ire. 1899-02 Surg/Lt BSAP Became Lt.Col. KCMG	HC
42	Lakie, William 1893 Farr/Mjr 620 BBP	Sub/Lt Vet.	K	Bech.	Bulawayo, Matabeleland 1896 Capt. Remount Dep. MRF	RC
43	Abbott, Edwin A. 1894 MMP 277	RSM	A 25	Eng.	Braemar Hse, Lancaster G. London W. 1896 Lt. MRF	HC
125	Adames, Ernest Gribbon	Tpr.	A 28	Eng.	Green Bank, Lewes, Sussex HC 1899-1900 Cpl. 539 BSAP D. Bulawayo 4.12.1899	
124	Adams, Harold Acton 1894 MMP 265	Tpr.	A 26	Eng.	8, Longford Pl. St. John's Wood, Lon. 1896 Tpr. MRF 1897 Rhodesian Horse	HC
129	Adkins, Clement 1895 MMP no. 259	Tpr,	A	C.C.	Fort Jackson, C.C.	RC
53	Adye, Sydney	L/Sgt.	K 28	Eng.	Mafeking, Bechuanaland	HC
126	Allen, Harry George W. Tpr. 1688 BBP	Tpr.	K 21	Eng.	Park St. Winchester, Glos. 1896 Tpr. MRF. D. 16.10.96	HC
127	Anthony, Lewis	Tpr.	K 25	Eng.	Mafeking, Bechuanaland	HC

128	Armstrong, James St.G.P Sgt. MMP 445	Tpr.	D 24	Ire.	Garry Cas. Bandghes, King's HC Co. Ire. 1896 Sgt. BSAP
80	Ashwin, Richard 1893 BBP. 1894 MMP 137	Cpl.	B 29	Eng.	Bretforton, Evesham, Worcs. HC 1896 TSM, MRF. D. 1938
132	Babb, Leonard	Tpr.	K 24	Eng.	Kimberley, Griqualand W. HC 1896 Tpr. MRF. 1914-18 No. A267 BSAP, E.Africa
81	Baker, Alfred Lee	Cpl.	B 20	Eng.	Redholme, Queen's Rd HC Richmond, Surrey
130	Bale, John BBP No. 2210. MMP 51 1893 SM Victoria Column	Tpr.	G 35	Eng.	116, Mead St. Bathbridge HC Bristol. 19.4.98 – 31.10.06 Tpr. 870 & 65 BSAP
133	Ballantine, James Doug.	Tpr.	C 22	Scot.	Bulawayo, Matabeleland HC 1899-02 Tpr. 812 BSAP
u/k	Ballard, W.F.	Cpl.	G		Escaped 1896, Tpr. MMP - 295. Some reports accidentally killed, no confirmation.
134	Barnes, Ernest	Tpr.	C 24	Eng.	Maplehurst, Kent. Wounded HC 1896. Tpr. MMP 318
486	Barnes, Edward G.	Sgt.		Eng.	3,Harwood Villas, Har- *Illovo* wood Rd. Merton, Surrey 1896 Tpr. Gwelo Vols. 1899-02 Sgt. 2406 BSAP
44	Bateson, Malcolm Weir 1893 MMP 163	Trp.SM	Art. 26	Eng.	Gargrave, via Leeds HC 1896 Sgt/M. MMP 441
504	Beadon, HGN Musgrave CMR.	Cpl.	CMR	E.	Tauntfield, Taunton, *Matabele* Somerset. Slightly wounded
135	Beale, William NMP 1885-87. CMR 1887-92. BBP 1892-95	Tpr.	G 22	Eng.	Mafeking, Bechuanaland HC 1896 MMP. 1896-1908 Tpr. 101/9 BSAP. D.22.9.30 Obit. Rhod. Rly. Review 1930
u/k	Beard, Seymour H. 1894 MMP	Cpl.	C		MMP. No. 275 Kia - c/o 10 Basinghall St London ec

No.	Name	Rank		Nat.	Details	
136	Belk, Samuel Waterhouse 1ST Class Army Reserve	Tpr.	D 27	Eng.	Kimberley, C.C. 1896 Tpr. MRF. 1899-02 Lt. KLH. Lt. KTG & Capt. Kimb.Horse	HC
82	Bellew, Charles Joseph 1st Class Army Reserve	Cpl.	G 27	Eng.	15, Kaye St. Halifax, Nova Scotia, Canada.	HC
137	Bennett, James Tpr. 1932 BBP	Tpr.	G 28	Eng.	Mossborough, Sheffield. 1899-02 Tpr. 818 BSAP	HC
138	Bernstein, Harry L. 1893, Lt. Raaf's Col. MMP no. 238	Tpr.	Art. 25	Aus.	56, Grey St. East Melbourne 1897-98 West African F.F.	HC
139	Berry, Ernest A.	Tpr.	B 27	Eng.	Southsea, England 1896 Tpr. MRF	HC
140	Bevan, Alfred Ernest	Tpr.	G 24	Eng.	Gaberones, Bechuanaland 1897 Tpr. MMP, no. 597	HC
141	Bewley, Edmund	Tpr.	C 20	Prussia	Bulawayo, Matabeleland	HC
142	Billing, Herbert Lindsey Tpr. 1636 BBP	Tpr.	G 33	Eng.	Gaberones, Bechuanaland 1896 Tpr. MRF '97 Tpr RHV	HC
--	Black, A. 1893 Tpr. Raaf's Col. MMP no. 452	Tpr.	A		Kia, buried Blaaubank Farm c/o Mrs M.C. Cokner, 29, Eldon Road. Kensington.	
143	Blankenberg, Charles Henry Tpr.	Tpr.	Art.	C.C.	Bulawayo, Matabeleland. 1895, MMP no. 311	RC
45	Blatherwick, James Kincaid Tr. SM		G	C.C.	77, Slope St. Cape Town 1896-1918 RSM, 185 & 20 DWS. 1918	RC
--	Bletsoe, John Bernard Tpr. MMP no. 343	Tpr.	B		Kia, buried Randfontein Grendon Hall, Northampton	
--	Bleular, G.	Tpr.	B		Missing. S/Insp. Chawner reported that this man deserted at first stop 25 miles from Pitsani	
54	Borrell, George 1893 Tpr. BBP no. 672	Sgt.	K 40	Switz	Mafeking, Bechuanaland 1896 Arm/Sgt. MRF. 1899-1902 Tpr. BSAP Died 8/2/1935 Gaberones	HC

83	Bourke, Thomas Edward 1893 MMP no. 200	Cpl.	G 25	Aus	Railway Rd, Malvern, Melbourne, Aus. BBP no.1743	HC
146	Bouwer, Cornelius F. 1893, BBP Tpr. No. 1809	Tpr.	Art.	C.C.	Grahamstowm, C.C.	RC
144	Bowden, Sydney V.	Tpr.	K 24	Scot.	Albany, Dumfries, Scotland	HC
55	Brady, Archibald Henry 1893 Sgt. BBP no. 1400	Sgt.	K	Natal	Mafeking, Bechuanaland *Durban* 1899-1902 Tpr. 2374 BSAP	
147	Brand, William John	Tpr.	C	C.C.	Bristol, C.C. 1896 Tpr. Sby. Field Force.	RC
148	Brennan, Francis Dawse 1890 BSACP	Tpr.	C 25	Eng.	Tamer Hse. St Mark's Rd. N. Kensington, London	HC
150	Broberg, John 1893 Tpr. BBP no.995	Tpr.	K 28	Swed.	Mafeking, Bechuanaland 1899-1902 Tpr. 2418 BSAP.	HC
149	Brooks, Montague T.	Tpr.	D 24	Eng.	158, Sinclair Rd., West Ken- ington, London.1896 Tpr.MRF	HC
56	Brown, Frederick Sheard	Sgt.	A 32	Scot.	11, Ann St. Edinburgh 1895, MMP no. 338	HC
157	Brown, Frederick W. 1895, Tpr. MMP no. 492	Tpr.	A 27	Eng.	High St. Borough, Ldn. SE. 1896 Tpr. MRF. 1914-18 BEA Labour Corps. Wia.	HC
--	Brown, Martin Woodham Attested MMP 7/10/1895	Tpr.	D		'Walnuts', Pen Keys Green, Maidenhead, Berks. Kia. MMP no. 427	
155	Browne, Richard J. 1893 Tpr. BBP	Tpr.	D	C.C.	82, Sir Lowry Rd. CapeTown 1896 Tpr. BSAP.	RC
490	Bruce, Stewart Army Reserve	Tpr.	D	Scot.	9 Avidon St. Dundee, Sc. *Inanda* Wounded 1896. Tpr MMP 416	
151	Bryan, Francis	Tpr.	C 25	Eng.	Hull, Yorkshire 1914-18 A263 BSAP S.R. Column, G.E.A.	HC
84	Bull, Henry Collins 1893 MMP 262	Cpl.	A 20	Eng.	Redhill, Surrey	HC

131	Bull, James	Tpr.	Art. Mat.	Holt, Norfolk	RC
152	Burgess, Arthur 1893 Tpr. 2100 BBP	Tpr.	K	C.C.	Grahamstown, C.C. 1896 Tpr. MMP. 1899-02 Tpr. No. 26 B. Sqn, Rhod. Reg. Mashonaland Hse. & SAC	RC
153	Burgess, William Robert 1893 Tpr. 989 BBP	Tpr.	K	C.C.	Grahamstown, C.C. 1896 Tpr. MMP	RC
145	Burke, John	Tpr.	A 25	Ire.	25, Strand St. Co. Galway, Ire. 1896 Tpr. MMP no. 399	HC
156	Burnands, John Arthur 7th Drgn. Gds. 1891 Tpr. 748 BSACP	Tpr.	Art. 27	Eng.	27, The Boltons, S. Kensin. London. 1896 Sgt. BSAP, no. 315. 1899-02 Sgt. 1239 Cape Rly.Sharpshooters. D. 4.8.63. Wia	HC
154	Burnside, Robert N.	Tpr.	A 20	Eng.	51, Keruer St. Stuttgart, Ger. 1895 Tpr. MMP, 105/335	HC
491	Burrows, Sampson M. 1893 L/Cpl 1836 BBP	Tpr.	A	Eng.	c/o T.Burrows,Hilder's *Pretoria* Brewery, Birmingham Sev. Wounded. MMP 158	
158	Calder, John Army Reserve	Tpr.	K 24	Scot.	Mafeking, Bechuanaland 1896 MMP no. 109	HC
159	Calderwood, John 1893 Tpr. 1718 BBP	Tpr.	B 26	Eng.	Bulawayo, Matabeleland BSACP no.825. 1894 MMP no. 284. D. 26.8.1899	HC
184	Callanan, Henry A. 1893 Tpr. 2014 BBP	Tpr.	D	C.C.	c/o James E. Mclusher, Graaf Reinet. 1899-02 Tpr. No. 43, A Sqn Rhod. Reg. Cpl. Warwick's Scouts	RC
160	Canton, Claude F.	Tpr.	A 18	Eng.	24 Upp.Wimpole St. Lon.W 1895 Tpr. 109	HC
u/k	Campbell, J.	Tpr.			Poss. 1885 BBP, also 1894 MMP no. 117	
161	Carlyle, Thomas	Tpr.	C 19	Eng.	Salisbury, Mashonaland 1896 MMP no. 132	HC

179	Carpenter, Frederick	Tpr.	Art. 32	Eng.	190, Clapham Rd. London 1896 MMP no. 410	HC
163	Carson, James G.	Tpr.	Art.	C.C.	Kingswilliamstown 1894 MMP 239. 1896 Tpr. MRF	RC
162	Carson, Thomas	Tpr.	A 26	Eng.	Cape Town 1896 MMP no. 387	HC
164	Cartwright, James Henry	Tpr.	K 24	Eng.	Collision St. Nottingham Eng. 1895 MMP no. 146	HC
177	Celliers, Daniel Henry 1893 Tpr. No.1739 BBP	Tpr.	A	C.C.	Robertson,, C.C. 1896 Cpl. MMP no. 563	RC
173	Chadborn, John Arthur 1895 MMP no. 342	Tpr.	Art. 26	Eng.	Old Hse, Wollan, nr Glouc- ester. 1896 Pay SM. MRF 1899-1900 Pvt. no.517 CP	HC
u/k	Chalke, G.A. No. 2286 BBP	Tpr.	K		Mia escaped. See Pitsani Account. 1896 Tpr. MRF	-
176	Champken, Frederick	Tpr.	B 32	Eng.	56, Victoria Rd. Walford 1896 Tpr. MRF. 1897 RHV	HC
85	Chattaway, Norman H. 1895 MMP no. 328	Cpl.	A 25	Eng.	Rotherwick Rect. Winchfield Hants. 1896 L/Cpl E Troop BFF. D. 3.1.1935	HC
175	Chawles, Edmund	Tpr.	A	C.C.	Port Elizabeth, C.C. 1896 Cpl. MMP. 1899-02 no.613 SRV & TMI	RC
168	Cheatter, Joseph	Tpr.	A 21	Eng.	7, Kelso Rd. Clarnedon Rd Leeds, Yorkshire 1895 MMP no. 377	HC
169	Christian, George M.	Tpr.	B 37	Eng.	Box 1239, J'Burg SAR 1895 MMP no. 428	HC
174	Clarendon, Sydney C.	Tpr.	D 28	Eng.	13, St John's St, Adelphi Strand, London	HC
57	Clarke, James W.	Sgt.	C 28	Eng.	None 1896-7 Tpr. Umtali Vols.	HC
178	Clarke, William Thomas 1893 Cpl. Victoria Col.	Tpr.	D 25	Eng.	Edgeware Rd, London 1893-96 Sgt. MMP no. 49	HC

58	Clements, Percy Brook 1884 10th R. Hussars 1893 Tpr. No. 1755 BBP	Sgt.	D 29	Eng.	3, Corchester Sq. London 1896-98 SM MRF no.246. 1899-02 CMR. SAMR (SWA 1915).retd. 1926 Major DAAG. D. 9/1946	HC
180	Cloete,John Henry	Tpr.	C	C.C.	Victoria West. MMP no.288 Attested 30.1.1895	RC
183	Close, Percival T.S.	Tpr.	K	C.C.	Kimberley C.C.	RC
-	Coghill, R.M.S. Tpr. no. 556 MMP	Tpr.	C		Mia, escaped, no further info. c/o Dr JG Coghill, Ventnor IOW	
46	Cole, Mansell Lawford	Tpr. SM	K	C.C.	Somerset East, C.C.	RC
167	Collins, Bernard	Tpr.	G	C.C.	Mafeking, Bechuanaland	RC
170	Comer, Frank 1895 MMP no. 379	Tpr.	A 27	Eng.	Blackford, Welmore, Weston super Mare, Somerset 1899-02 Pte CP D2	HC
181	Constable, Hugh C.	Tpr	Art. 21	Eng.	7 Eaton Cres. Clifton Bristol 1896-1900 MMP. Sgt. no. 479, BSAP.	HC
171	Cook, Robert	Tpr.	A 20	Eng.	Bishop Wilton, Yorkshire 1896 Tpr. no. 367 MMP.	HC
86	Cooke, George Alfred 1893 Tpr. no.1671 BBP	Cpl.	G 22	Eng.	Mafeking, Bechuanaland 1896 Tpr. no. 255 MMP	HC
165	Cooper, Daniel Ernest	Tpr.	G 27	Aus.	Fairholme, Bexley Heath . Kent, 1896 Tpr. MRF	HC
59	Cottrell, Alfred George	Sgt.	G 25	Eng.	Athenian Villa, Stapleton Rd. Bristol. 1896-97 TSM no.89 BSAP. 1902/3 no.1334 BSAP	HC
166	Couser, Richard	Tpr.	K 20	Ire.	Melville Hse, Armagh	HC
172	Cozens, Arthur 1890 no.515 BSACP	Tpr.	D	Mat.	White Sq. Clapham, London 1894 MMP no. 281; 1895 BBP no. 1880	RC
182	Croft, Alfred, W.W.	Tpr.	K 42	Eng.	Blundellsands, Liverpool England	HC

60	Cumming, Adam Bennett 1893 Tpr. BBP no. 1986	Sgt.	B 24	Scot.	Craig Lea, Stirling, Scotl. 1894 TSM MMP no. 113 1899-02 BSAP att. Rh. Reg.	HC
185	Davey, Thomas William 1895 MMP no. 415	Tpr.	Art.	C.C.	Port Elizabeth. 1896 Cpl. B Trp. Belingwe Col. 1899-02 Tpr. SRV no. 571	RC
	Davidson, George J. 1895 MMP	Farr/Cpl	K		Mia, escaped, no further info. D. 6.8.1896	
62	Davies, Henry Markham MMP, no. 230	Sgt.	A	C.C.	c/o Radford, Shangani, Mat. 1896 TSM MMP. 1899-02 BSAP no. 1130	RC
u/k	Davies, Harry 1894 BBP no.1893. MMP no. 29	Tpr.			Kia, buried Randfontein	-
61	Davis, Gordon 1893 Cpl. Sby. Hse. MMP no. 7	Sgt.	D	Mat.	Selukwe, Matabeleland 1896 Sgt. MMP no. 587	RC
189	Day/Davy, Daniel	Tpr.	K 26	Eng.	Mafeking, Bechuanaland	HC
190	De la Haye, Francis M.	Tpr.	D	C.C.	6, Wells Sq. Cape Town 1896 Gnr.BFF. MMP /8-10/96	RC
187	De Legh, William Owen 1893 Tpr. BBP no.1790	Tpr.	G 24	Eng.	Bryanstone, Seaton, Devon 1896 Cpl. MRF. 1896-1919 TSM/Lt. BSAP nos. 212/11 Awarded DCM. D. 26.8.51	HC
492	Den, Malcolm	Tpr.	A	C.C.	Sea Point, Cape Town *Mexican* 1896 Tpr. MRF. Stly.wounded	
191	Devereaux, Lawrence 1895 MMP no. 134	Tpr.	C 21	Eng.	Somerville Cross Ave, Booterstown, Dublin	HC
87	Dewar, Arthur Robert J. 92nd Highlanders	Cpl.	B 26	Eng.	1, St George's Tce. Ryde IOW. 1895 MMP	HC
88	Dobbyn, Thomas 1893 L/Cpl. BBP no.1576 1894 MMP no. 219	Cpl.	Art. 32	Aus.	Bulawayo, Matabeleland 1896 Sgt. MMP no. 661 23.11.1898 – 13.10.04 Sgt. BSAP nos.943/74	HC

63	Dobson, Joseph Gord. V. 1893 L/Cpl BBP 1325	L/Sgt	K 30	Eng.	Mafeking, Bechuanaland HC 1896 Sig. Sgt. MRF. 1899-01 TSM BSAP no. 335. 1901 BNP
u/k	Dodge, James Horsfield	Tpr.	B		Mia, escaped. See Pitsani Account under Wodge. 1896 MMP no. 307 1899-02 Sgt. Rimington's Scouts
64	Douglas, Frank Arthur	Sgt.	G	C.C.	c/o J. Forman,Esq. The Park RC Nottingham
89	Doyle, Ashley Crofton 1893 Tpr. BBP no. 1766	Cpl.	A 27	Eng.	Dacre Hse, Lee, Kent HC 1896 Sgt. MRF
488	Dreyer, Frederick W.	Cpl.	A	Nam.	Pt. Nolloth, Namaqual. *Norman* See Pitsani Acc. Sev. Wounded. MMP 182
186	Driver, Percy Erskine T. 1894 MMP no. 434	Tpr.	C 26	Ire.	c/o Mrs D.E. Fitz'd-Murray HC Stour Hill, Co. Tyrone 1899-02 Tpr. BSAP 1061
90	Dumaresq, Rawlins	Cpl.	B 26	Eng.	St. Peter's Port, Guernsey HC CI. 1896 SM MRF. 1897- 1921 SM/Capt. BSAP 371/30 Wia. D.1950
188	Du Plooy, Rudolph	Tpr.	G	C.C.	Kimberley, Griqualand W. RC
195	Eames, Thomas Banbury Lt. 3rd Batt. Connaught R.	Tpr.	A 22	Eng.	1,Chichester Rd. Chester HC England
192	Early, Frederick	Tpr.	B	C.C.	Mafeking, Bechuanaland RC 1896 Tpr. MRF. 1899-02 Tpr. BSAP no. 882
193	Eastwood, Francis E. Lt. 5th Batt R. Fusiliers	Tpr.	Art. 24	Eng.	Ormand H. Ryde IOWight HC 1896 Lt.MRF. Wia 29.7.96 1897 Lt.RHV. 1899-02 Lt. BSAP. D. 26.8.1932
u/k	Edgecombe. Tpr. MMP no. 550	Tpr.	D		Mia, escaped, no further info.
u/k	Edwards, D. MMP no. 488	Tpr.	B		Died, buried Vlakfontein Farm

194	Elliot, Richard J. 1893. Tpr. 1706 BBP	Tpr.	G 25	Eng.	Clay Hill, Enfield 1896 Tpr. MRF	HC
u/k	Evans	Tpr.			Kia. Buried Violet Mine. Not listed Gaberones Archives Lists	
196	Fabing, Lancelot Matthew	Tpr.	A 19	Eng.	Worm Leighton, Leamington 1899-02 Cpl. CMP Div. 2	HC
91	Farmery Edwin Armistead 1890 BSACP 1893 BBP no. 1464	Cpl.	C 26	Eng.	Harrogate, Yorkshire 1896 QM/Sgt. MRF	HC
198	Farrell, Edward O'Connell 1890 Pioneers.1893 Lt. Vic.Col.	Tpr.	B 49	Ire.	Bulawayo, Matabeleland	HC
197	Farrell, Michael George 1893 Lt Vic. Col. BBP no. 1855	Tpr.	D	C.C.	26, Wicht St. Cape Town 1894 MMP no. 96. 1896 Tpr. MRF	RC
207	Fenton, Frederick Arthur 4th Drgn Gds. 1895 MMP no. 437	Tpr.	C 23	Eng.	Mount Rose, Tutshill,Chep- stow. 1896 Sgt. MRF	HC
201	Finch, William	Tpr.	K 28	Eng.	Mafeking, Matabeleland 1896 Tpr. MRF	HC
204	Flynn, John J.	Tpr.	C 26	Eng.	Vryburgh, Bechuanaland 1896 Tpr. MRF. 1899-02 Tpr. BSAP no.1028	HC
199	Forsyth, Alfred Burnet 1893 BBP no.1546 MMP no. 188	Tpr.	Art.	C.C.	Mowbray, C.C. Mid. Kia. Tafelkop 20.1.01. 1896 Cpl. MMP. 1897 Tpr. Mt. Darwin Vols. 1899-00 Tpr. BSAP no.134 1901 Darn'ts Hse. No.39281	RC
u/k	Forster (Foster) John RH 2nd Yorks & Lancs no. 2178 1893 Tpr. Vic. Col.	Tpr.	D		Kia 2.1.96 buried Randfontein Tpr. MMP no. 549. c/o James Forster, 90 Bygove St. North St. Poplar, London E.	
205	Foxcroft, Richard 1894 MMP 216	Tpr.	B	Ofs.	Ficksburg, OFS	*Durban*
206	Francis, William Clarence 1893 Tpr. BBP no.1979	Tpr.	B	C.C.	Kimberley, C.C. 1896 Tpr. MMP no. 81 1899-01 Tpr. BSAP no.1018	RC

203	Franklin, Benjamin Charles. MMP no. 273	Tpr.	A	C.C.	Worcester, C.C. 1896 Tpr. MMP. 1897-01 Tpr. BSAP no.786. D. Monze 30.04.01	RC
200	Fraser, James John Meintjes	Tpr.	B	C.C.	Beaufort West. 1899-02 believed to be no.1203 BSAP	RC
u/k	Fraser, David 1893 Tpr. no. 1459 BBP	Tpr.	G		Dow. Buried Krugersdorp 10.1.96. Son of Gen. Sir David Fraser, The Grange, Castle Connell, Limerick, Ireland	
u/k	Friedman, E.H. BBP no. 1650	Tpr.	K		Mia. Escaped. 1896 Tpr. E Troop, BFF	
202	Frost, John 1895 MMP no. 375	Tpr.	Art. 26	Eng.	Sand, Wedmore, Weston-super-Mare, Somerset. 1896 Tpr. MRF	HC
493	Fyvie, Dermir McFarlane 1895 MMP no. 421	Tpr.	A	Natal	c/o HD Fyvie, Hathorn *Durban* & Mason, Pietermaritzburg. Seriously wdd: 1899-02 Tpr. BSAP no. 933 & Steinakers Horse.	
213	Gall, John	Tpr.	A 26	Scot.	24, Hayburn Cres. Partick Glasgow. 1896 Tpr. MRF	HC
221	Garcia, Egbert Morris 1895 Tpr. MMP no. 306	Tpr.	A	C.C.	Kingswilliamstown 1896 Tpr. MRF	RC
208	Gardiner, Alexander W. 1895 Tpr. MMP no. 373	Tpr.	B 24	Scot.	25, Gladstone St. Glasgow 1896 Tpr. MRF. 1897 Umtali Volunteers.	HC
215	Gardyne, Thomas McLoud Bruce. MMP no.364	Tpr.	D 22	Eng.	None 1896 Cpl. MRF	HC
214	Gettliffe, Simon	Tpr.	A	C.C.	Cape Town	RC
65	Gibb, David 1894 MMP no. 246	Sgt.	A 21	Scot.	c/o J Gibbs, 24 Stirling Rd Galashields, Scotland. 1896 QM Sgt. MRF	HC
92	Gibb, William 1894 MMP no. 245	Cpl.	Art. 25	Scot.	Galashields, Scotland. 1896 Sgt. MRF. Kia 5.8.96	HC

222	Gibbs, Henry C. 1890 Tpr. BSACP	Tpr.	A	C.C.	Albert Rd. Woodstock, C.C. RC Reg. no. 482. Slightly wounded
218	Gibbs, Joseph W.	Tpr.	A	C.C.	Albert Rd, Woodstock, C.C. RC 1896 Tpr. RHV. wia 9/96 1899-1902 Tpr. SRV
209	Gibson, William Mitchell 1893 Tpr. BBP no. 1491	Tpr.	K	C.C.	Mafeking, Bechuanaland. RC 1896 Tpr. MMP
217	Gilmore, Robert	Tpr.	K 26	Ire.	Mafeking, Bechuanaland. HC 1896 Cpl. MRF
211	Going, Gerald H.	Tpr.	G	Bech.	Mafeking, Bechuanaland RC 1899-02 Tpr. BSAP no. 2412 Wia 31.3.1900
216	Gooch, Brook	Tpr.	C 27	Eng.	England. HC 1896 Tpr. MRF. 1902 SRCons.
220	Gordon, Thomas	Tpr.	D	C.C.	27, Plein St. Cape Town RC 1896 Tpr.MMP Wia 5.8.96 1899-02 Tpr. no. 629 SRV, & NPMR
223	Gorringe, Leonard Reg. no. 569	Tpr.	D 22	Eng.	Kingston by Sea, Sussex HC Wia. Capt. Sudan Police. MC WWI. D.6.1.1941, Nairobi See Obit. East African Std. Papers NAM ref. 8218/19.
219	Gray, Cecil Alexander	Tpr.	A 25	Eng.	Healy Grove, Burnley,Lancs HC 1896 Tpr .MRF. 1899-02 Tpr. Rhod. Reg. 437
210	Green, George Army Res. Pvt. 3rd Drag.Gds	Tpr.	K 29	Eng.	Mafeking, Bechuanaland HC 1896 Sgt. MRF. 1896-09 Sgt. BSAP nos. 108/12
93	Grieves, Cecil Goldsmid Army Res. Royal Drgns	Cpl.	K 24	Eng.	266 Canonbury Pk Rd., HC Norberton, Surrey. 1896 Sgt. MMP no.337
94	Grimes, Gordon Henry	L/Cpl.	K 21	Eng.	Knapton Hall, North HC Walsam, Norfolk
212	Gunn, Angus Donald	Tpr.	D 25	Scot.	Cullen, Banffshire, Scot. HC 1896 Tpr. MRF 1899-02 Tpr. SRV no. 100

231	Hackvale, Arthur Edward	Tpr.	D 29	Eng.	Umtali, Mashonaland 1896 Tpr. MRF	HC
245	Haddingham, William	Tpr.	B 24	Eng.	8, Fernleigh, Rainham Rd. Upp. Edmonton, London 1896 Tpr. MMP no. 477	HC
226	Haggblad, Emil	Tpr.	B 29	Swe.	Gruskooruswek, Sweden 1897 Tpr. MRF no. 139	HC
u/k	Hall BBP no. 2169	Tpr.	K		Mia. Escaped. No further information.	
224	Handley, Herbert Humphrey	Tpr.	K	C.C.	Molteno, C.C.	RC
244	Handsomebody,William Harvey	Tpr.	G 25	Eng.	Mafeking, Bechuanaland	HC
225	Hanley, Joseph	Tpr.	A 27	Ire.	25, Mallow St. Limerick 1899-02 Tpr. Rhod. R. no.396	HC
241	Harber, Walter Alexander 1895 MMP no. 403	Tpr.	A 21	Eng.	10, Pittbille Villas, Chelten- ham. 1896 Tpr. MRF. 1897 MMP no. 765	HC
96	Harrington, Charles Herbert 1895 MMP no. 436	Cpl.	C 21	Eng.	6, Cardigan Rd. Richmond	HC
240	Harris, Charles Henry 1895 MMP no. 356	Tpr.	C 27	Eng.	Tuli, Matabeleland 1896 Tpr. MRF	HC
243	Harris, Reginald Oke. Army Reservist	Tpr.	B 27	Eng.	Holloway Rd. Exeter 1896 TSM MRF	HC
235	Harrison, Edward Hyde	Tpr.	G 22	Eng.	20, Westbourne Tce, Hyde Park, London. 1897 Tpr. BSAP no.462	HC
95	Harwood, Evelyn Gwynne	L/Cpl.	G 23	Eng.	23, Bath Rd. Bedford Park West. 1896 Cpl. MRF. 1899-02 Tpr. SRV no. 745 MMP no. 107. D. 6.1.1900	HC
232	Hatherell, John E. 1895 MMP no. 423	Tpr.	B 25	Eng.	Elem Grove, Chipping Sudbury, Gloucester	HC

237	Hay, Edward James 1894 MMP no. 271. 1895 no. 425	Tpr.	B 26	Ire.	Bulawayo, Matabeleland 1896 Cpl. MRF. 1899-02 Tpr. BSAP no. 700	HC
494	Hayes, Frederick A.	Tpr.	C	Eng.	Marlborough, Wiltshire *Inanda* Wia.	
66	Hector, John 1893 L/Cpl BBP no. 1985	Sgt.	B 25	Scot.	4, Cherry Bank, Aberdeen Scotland. 1894 MMP no.161. 1896 SM MRF	HC
u/k	Hennessy, C.E. Tpr. MMP no. 547	Tpr.	D		Kia. 2.1.96.Buried Randfontein c/o Mrs Hennessy, Tintern, Chepstow, England.	
234	Herbert, Percy William		D	Eng.	Bulawayo, Matebeleland 1896 Sgt. MRF. D. 15.11.1896	HC
47	Hill, Charles William King SM 1893 Tpr. BBP no. 1674 MMP no. 104		A 22	Eng.	Bulawayo, Matabeleland 1896 SM MRF. 1899-1900 TSM BSAP no. 279. 1901-02 Lt. KFS	HC
218	Hill, John Hall Tpr. CMR. 1893 Cpl. BBP no. 1803	Tpr.	A 34	Eng.	22, Mecklenburgh Sq. Lon. 1894 MMP no.168. 1896 Tpr. MRF.	HC
230	Hill, Phillip Leonard 1895 MMP no. 308	Tpr.	B 27	Eng.	5, The Linders, Reading	HC
229	Hillary, James 1893 Tpr. BBP no. 1944	Tpr.	D	C.C.	5, Lee Street, Cape Town 1896 Tpr. MRF.	RC
233	Holloway, Frank Vivian 1895 MMP no. 406	Tpr.	D 31	NZ.	Bulawayo 1896 Cpl. Sby. Field Force	HC
228	Holmes, Alfred J.	Tpr.	K 22	Eng.	Mafeking, Bechuanaland 1896 Tpr. MRF	HC
u/k	Holt, Charles John Tpr. MMP no. 553	Tpr.	D		39, Williams St. Cape Town Mia, escaped. 1896 SFF. See Pitsani Account	.
239	Hooper, James 1893 Tpr. BBP no. 1116	Tpr.	C 34	USA.	Bulawayo, Matabeleland 1894 MMP no. 154. 1896 Tpr. MRF.	HC

u/k	Horsford, Knightly O'B. Army Res. 1895 MMP 359	Tpr.	A	Eng.	11, Cornwallis Cres. Clifton D. Mafeking. 31.8.1896	HC
227	Hoseason, Cecil de C.S. Army. Res. E Surrey R.	Tpr.	K 27	Eng.	4, York Cr.Rd Clifton Bristol	HC
67	Hosken, Charles Cuthbert Fayrer.1894 MMP no. 235	Sgt.	B 20	Scot.	12a, Charterhouse Sq. Lond. 1896 TSM Rh. Hse. 1897-99 Lt. BSAP. 1914-21 Lt. Col. Middlesex Regt. 1939 Lt. Col. Home Guard.	HC
u/k	Hutchinson, WJC Tpr. MMP no. 368	Tpr.	B		Dow, buried Vkalfontein, c/o Col. Stevenson, 36 Montpelier Villas, Cheltenham, Eng.	
236	Hyman, Raleigh	Tpr.	C	C.C.	Belmont Hse Somerset Rd, Cape Town	RC
246	Ibbs, Charles Henry	Tpr.	K 30	Eng.	Mafeking, Bechuanaland 1896 Tpr. MRF. 1902 SRC	HC
97	Ingham, John Seager Lt. 4th Gloucs. 1895 MMP no. 319	Cpl.	D 23	Eng.	3, Hayes Rd. Bath, Eng. 1896 Cpl MMP. 1899-1918 Lt. BSAP. Served GEA. D. 29.8.41	HC
254	Jack, Robert 1893 Tpr. MMP 1968	Tpr.	A	C.C.	c/o Isaac's Mafeking 1895 MMP no. 399. 1896 Tpr. MRF.	RC
252	Jackson, Henry Barrett 1895 MMP no. 380	Tpr.	A 22	Eng.	Rosebury Ave. London	HC
253	Jackson, Henry	Tpr.	A 22	Eng.	Main St. St Bees, England 1896 Tpr. MRF	HC
251	Jackson, Robert 1894 MMP no. 241	Tpr.	Art. 24	Eng.	Tyson Rd. Forest Hill, Lon. '95 MMP 293. '96 Cpl. MRF.	HC
250	James, Edward Henry 1895 MMP no. 133	Tpr.	C	C.C.	Cape Town	RC
258	Jardine, Cecil A.	Tpr.	B 20	Eng.	15 Baskerville Rd. Wandsworth, London	HC
248	Jenkins, Alexander Jameson 1893 Tpr. BBP no. 2087	Tpr.	Art.	C.C.	Barkley East MMP no. 199	RC

247	Jennings, Arthur	Tpr.	K	C.C.	Grahamstown	RC
					1899-1902 possibly Tpr.	
					no. 2583. J.A.	

259	Johnson, George	Tpr.	K	Eng.	Mafeking, Bechuanaland	HC
	West Riding Regt.		23		1896 Tpr. MRF. 1896-1905	
					Tpr. BSAP no. 13. Dws	

255	Johnstone, Tom Robert	Tpr.	C	Eng.	48, Bromley Rd. Beckenham HC	
	Cartlege Harrison.		29		Kent. 1896-1909 Sgt. BSAP	
	Lt. 1st Batt. Hampshire Regt.				no. 571 & 22.	
	IGS				D. Byo. 1909. BSA, QSA, KSA	
					& 1902 Coronation Medals	

256	Johnstone, George Hugh	Tpr.	D	Eng.	The Lines, Braintree, Essex	HC
			23		1896 Cpl. MRF. 1899-1902	
					Tpr. SRV, B Troop no. 78	

249	Jones, Francis Alfred	Tpr.	B	Eng.	Tynyfro, Crickhowel,	HC
	1894 MMP no. 164		25		Brecon, Wales. 1896 Tpr. MRF	
					1899-02 SM BSAP no.1342	

257	Jones, William H.E.	Tpr.	C	Eng.	Grammer Hall, Fakenham,	HC
	1893 Tpr. Raaf's Col.		25		Norfolk. 1896 Sgt. K Tpr.	
					Byo. F.F.	

| 98 | Jupp, Richard Barry | Cpl. | A | Eng. | Royal Hospital, Chelsea | HC |
| | 1893 Tpr. BBP no.1418 | | 26 | | 1896 TSM MRF no.443 | |

| 260 | Kallenborn, John B. | Tpr. | D | C.C. | Mafeking, Bechuanaland | RC |
| | | | | | 1896 Tpr. MMP | |

| 266 | Kavanagh, Thomas E. | Tpr. | D | Eng. | The Cedars, Colchester, | HC |
| | | | 24 | | Essex. 1896 Tpr. MMP 637 | |

| u/k | Kebz/Keltz, W.C. | Tpr. | D | | Mia .Escaped. See Pitsani Acc. | |

267	Keenan, Percy Walker	Tpr.	B	Eng.	210, Upland Rd, E.Dulwich,	HC
			19		London. 1897-1902	
					Cpl. BSAP nos. 721/988	

| u/k | Kelsall, William H. | Tpr. | C | | Mia. Escaped. See Pitsani Acc. | |
| | MMP no. 527 | | | | 1896 Tpr. MRF | |

| 262 | Kennedy, Leslie C. | Tpr. | C | Eng. | 21, St. Margaret St., | HC |
| | Coleridge | | 22 | | Liverpool. 1896 Tpr. MRF | |

261	Kenny, John J.	Tpr.	C	C.C.	Walner Rd. Port Elizabeth 1896 MMP no .381	RC
264	Kenny, John	Tpr.	D 19	Eng.	Mafeking, Bechuanaland	HC
265	Kerr, Fred. C.J.	Tpr.	A 24	Scot.	14, Hartingdon Pl. Edinburgh. 1896 Tpr. MRF	HC
263	Keyes, William	Tpr.	D	C.C.	Bulawayo, Matabeleland	RC
268	King, Joseph George 1893, Tpr. Victoria Col.	Tpr.	A	C.C.	c/o Walter Bain, Loot Kraal, Bulawayo. 1893 MMP No. 71/209. 1896 Tpr. MRF.	RC
269	Kirby, Lewis J. 1894 MMP no. 179	Tpr.	Art. 25	Eng.	St. James Pl. London	HC
270	Kirk, Charles James	Tpr.	K 22	NZ.	Mafeking, Bechuanaland 1896 Tpr. MRF	HC
u/k	Kirkpatrick, W.J. Tpr. MMP no. 362	Tpr.	B		Wia. Escaped, reported Bulawayo Chronicle. See Pitsani Account. 1896 Gwelo Vols.	
271	Laidlaw, James Bruce 1895 MMP no. 412	Tpr.	A 23	Eng.	Ryton, Wallington, Surrey	HC
283	Lalor, John Lardener 1895 MMP no. 376	Tpr.	B 20	Ire.	Gaol St. Enniscorthy, Co. Clare.	HC
u/k	Lamb, George Bellfield Louis	Tpr.	G		Kia.Buried Krugersdorp 2.1.96 c/o H.E. Lamb, Wentworthy, Devon, England	
274	Lang, George 1893 Tpr. Sby. Hse.	Tpr.	D	Mash	Glasgow, Scotland 1896 Tpr. MMP	RC
275	Langton, Courtney 1895 MMP no. 383	Tpr.	B 30	Eng.	Bulawayo, Matabeleland 1896 Tpr. A Troop MMP. Kia 6.7.96.	HC
276	Langworthy, Harry W.	Tpr.	A 21	Eng.	Brook Ho. Modbury, Devon	HC
u/k	Larson, John Oscar	Tpr.	B		Missing, believed escapee. 1894 MMP no. 206	

285	Law, William 1893 Tpr. BBP no. 2075	Tpr.	K 35	Eng.	69, Standley Rd. Liverpool 1896 Tpr., Gifford's Horse	HC
272	Lawlor, Edward James	Tpr.	C 21	Eng.	Berkshire, England	HC
281	Lawrie, James S.	Tpr.	D 24	Scot.	31, Geoffrey St. Edinburgh	HC
69	Lawson, Charles Frederick 1894 MMP no. 222	Sgt.	A 31	Eng.	No add. 1896 MMP no. 444 1896 Tpr. MRF. 1899-1902 Lt. KLH.	HC
99	Leary, Edward Army Res. Cpl. 3rd Drgs	Cpl.	K 30	Eng.	Mafeking, Bechuanaland 1896 Sgt. MMP no. 187	HC
68	Lester, Charles Reginald	Sgt.	A	Eng.	22, Amesbury Ave. Streat- ham Hill, Lon.1896 SSM MMP	HC
282	Lewis, Alfred 1895 MMP no. 809	Tpr.	B	Eng.	Bulawayo, Matabeleland 1896 Tpr. MRF	HC
273	Lewis, Edward Charles	Tpr.	B	Eng.	Armour Rd, Tilehurst, Reading.	HC
280	Lewis, James George	Tpr.	B 31	Ire.	Bandon, Co. Cork. 1896 Tpr. MRF	HC
277	Lister, Edward Henry Cecil 1895 MMP no. 302	Tpr.	B 22	Eng.	Warren Lodge, Newmarket	HC
70	Little, Hugh Mervyn	Sgt.	C 22	Eng.	4, The Crescent, Mount Rad- ford. Exeter. 1896 Sgt. BSAP no. 187	HC
286	Logan, George exBomb'r RA. BBP no. 2255	Tpr.	K 27	Scot.	Cairn Villa, Auckmill, Aber- deen. 1896 Tpr. MMP	HC
100	London, William C. 1890 BSACP no. 266 & BBP	Cpl.	A	Mat.	Bulawayo, Matabeleland 1894 MMP no.266. D. 26.5.96	RC
278	Low, Peter Pte. Army Reserve	Tpr.	D 36	Scot.	21, Abercrombie Pl. Stirling Scot. 1896 Tpr. MRF	HC
284	Lucy, Frederick Lionel	Tpr.	K 22	Eng.	20, Downfield Rd. Clifton Bristol. 1896 Tpr. MMP. D.1951	HC
279	Lundgren, Alfred John 1893 Tpr. BBP no. 1148	Tpr.	Art.	C.C.	Bulawayo, Matabeleland 1895 MMP no. 357 1897-02 Tpr .BSAP no.570.	HC

489	Lynn, Thomas Russell 1895 Cpl.MMP no.334	Cpl.	Art.	Scot.	Livingstone Tce Gallashiels Scotland. Dow Addington Hosp. Durban, 24.2.1896	--
320	Mack, William 1895 Tpr. BBP no.1000	Tpr.	Art.	C.C.	c/o H. Mack, Grahamstown 1894 MMP no. 274	RC
48	Mageean, Lowens Ernest 1893 Tpr. BBP no. 1754	SM	A 23	Ire.	c/o McIldowrie, Tudor Gdns Belfast. 1894 MMP no.172. 1896 Lt. MRF.	HC
304	Major, George	Tpr.	C 31	Ire.	Ballinderry, Aukin. 1896 Tpr. MRF	HC
316	Mallalieu, Joseph Pashley 1893 Tpr. BBP no. 1753	Tpr.	D 27	Eng.	Longside, Manchester 1894 MMP no. 250. Cpl. MRF	HC
u/k	Maloney, Cecil H. Tpr. MMP no. 533	Tpr.	A		Kia. Buried Krugersdorp 27.1.'96	
u/k	Manning, John 1894 Tpr. MMP no. 166	Tpr.	D		Mia. Escaped. See Pitsani Acc. 1896 Tpr. Art. Tr. 1897 Tpr.SRV	
287	Marchant, Edward	Tpr..	C 40	Eng.	2, Town St. Shepton Mallet	HC
297	Marchant, John	Tpr.	D	C.C.	Cape Town 1896-97 Sgt. BSAP no. 801	RC
u/k	Maree, James 1893 BBP no. 1992 Cpl. MMP nos. 134/426	Cpl.	C		Dow. Buried Doornkop c/o PO Box 1067, Johannesburg, SAR	
102	Marks, Clifford Webber 1894 MMP no. 195	Cpl.	A 22	Eng.	60/61 Mark Lane, London 1895 MMP no. 309	HC
306	Maroney, Patrick W.	Tpr.	D 25	NSW	GPO Cape Town 1896 Cpl. MRF. 1914-1918 2nd Rhod. Regt.	HC
294	Martin, Herbert James	Tpr.	B 21	Eng.	43, King's Rd Cambridge 1896 Tpr/Cpl 183/678 & 43 BSAP. D. 4.7.61	HC
101	Mattison, James Arthur	L/Cpl.	K 31	Eng.	Laurel Ho. Walkington Bev. erley, Yorkshire. 1896 Cpl. Sby. FF. 1897 Tpr. Garrison Vols.	HC

305	McAdam, John C. 1890 Tpr. BSACP. BBP 2130	Tpr.	K	C.C.	Port Elizabeth 1897 MMP no. 201	RC
303	McBarnett, Donald McP.	Tpr.	K 24	Eng.	c/o JK Lindsay, W.S. 16, Queen St., Edinburgh. 1896 Tpr. MRF. 1899-1902 Tpr. Rhod. Regt. no. 521	HC
u/k	McCarthy, Harry Francis BBP. No. 1027	Tpr.	G		Detained at Pretoria by SAR Ex-member Staats Artillery. 1899-1901 BSAP no. 1060	
71	McCracken, Burnett deCrez 1894 MMP no. 263	Sgt.	A 20	Eng.	38 Queen St. Cannon St. London.1896 Ord. SM MMP. 1898 Lt. BSAP Kia 9.11.1899	HC
302	McCullum, John Wallace	Tpr.	K 27	Scot.	Mafeking, Bechuanaland 1896 Tpr. MRF	HC
291	McGowan, William 1895 MMP no. 129	Tpr.	C	C.C.	Port Elizabeth, C.C.	RC
314	McKenzie, George S. 1893 Tpr. Sby. Hse.	Tpr.	C 24	Scot.	Aultbea, Rosshire	HC
315	McKinley, Alexander S.	Tpr.	A 25	Scot.	St. James's St. Glasgow 1896 Tpr. MRF	HC
105	McLachlan, William M. 1894 MMP no. 276	Cpl.	A 28	Eng.	c/o F.Richardson, 28 Fenchurch St. London. Wia. 1897 MMP no. 555. 1899-1902 Rhod. Regt. no.202	HC
317	McLean, James Angus Campbell	Tpr.	A 23	Eng,	14, Ethel Rd. Aiston Hse. London. 1896 Tpr. MRF. 1897 MMP no. 620	HC
103	McMahon, Robert Donald 1894 MMP no. 240	L/Cpl.	G	Eng.	Bulawayo, Matabeleland 1896 Tpr. MRF no. 589. 1899-02 Sgt. no. 393 B Sqn. Rhod. Regt. & SAC.	RC
307	McMillan, Donald Bather.	Tpr.	C	C.C.	Somerset West, C.C. 1896 Tpr. MRF. 1899-02 Cpl. BSAP no. 1100	RC
318	McMullin, Samuel 1890 BSACP no.379	Tpr.	D	Bech.	Gwelo, Matabeleland 1894 MMP no. 194	RC

292	McNamara, James	Tpr.	D	C.C.	Walmer, Port Elizabeth 1896 Tpr. MMP no. 832	RC
496	McVety, James 1895 MMP no. 357	Tpr.	D	C.C.	Oldham Rd. Manchester *Inanda* Wounded. 1896 Tpr. MRF	
289	Medcalfe, George Frederick T.	Tpr.	B	C.C.	Stellenbosch 1896 Tpr. Gwelo Dist. Vols.	RC
310	Meinne, John M. 19th Hussars	Tpr.	B 35	Scot.	Mafeking, Bechuanaland 1896 Tpr. MRF	HC
288	Menheniot, George 1894 MMP no. 205	Tpr.	A 35	Eng.	Helstone, Cornwall 1896 Cpl. MRF. 1899-02 1st ILH, 1st Sc. Hse. & Colonial Scouts.	HC
300	Merry, George Alexander	Tpr.	K 25	Eng.	Mafeking, Bechuanaland 1896 Tpr. MRF. 1899-1902 Lt. BSAP	HC
u/k	Meyers, J. Carl 1894 MMP no. 203	Tpr.	C		Mia, escaped. See Pitsani Acc.	
104	Mitchell, John Bentley 1890 BSACP no. 53	Cpl.	K	C.C.	c/o Standard Bank, Cape T. 1896 Sgt. Med. Staff Corps 1897 Tpr. MRF. Dow 27.6.97	HC
308	Moller, Henry Peter 1896 MMP no. 333	Tpr.	K	C.C.	Cape Town 1896 Tpr. MRF. 1897-1902 Tpr. BSAP 620/36	RC
301	Moloney, James A. Cecil 1893 MMP no. 395	Tpr.	A 32	Ire.	Bulawayo, Matabeleland 1896 Sgt. MRF. 1897 Sgt. Rhod. Hse. Vols.	HC
296	Monk, Ernest Wreland	Tpr.	D 22	NZ	Bulawayo, Matabeleland 1896 Tpr. MRF	HC
106	Moore, Alfred Henry	Cpl.	A 24	Eng.	2, Farrant St. Queens Park, London, W.	HC
312	Moore, Edward F. 1895 MMP no. 391	Tpr.	A 27	Eng.	Exmouth, Devon	HC
107	Moore, George	L/Cpl.	K 25	Eng.	Elinley Castle, nr. Pershore Worcs. 1899-1904 Cpl. BSAP nos. 1025 & 91.	HC

311	Moore, Percy Harold Evelyn	Tpr.	A 23	Eng.	Bulawayo, Matabeleland 1896 Sgt. MRF. 1896-98 Sgt. BSAP no. 540. 1899-02 A Sqn ILH no. 599. Latterly comm-ıssioned. D. Durban 4.7.1956	HC
	1893 Tpr. Vic. Column 1894 Tpr. MMP no. 57					
290	Moras, Eugene	Tpr.	A 23	USA	Livingstone, Park County, Montana, USA	HC
298	Moreland, Henry 1895 MMP no. 372	Tpr.	B 21	Eng.	Pegswood Colliery, North-umberland. 1896 Tpr. MRF	HC
295	Morgan, James Edwards 1893 Tpr. BBP no. 2146	Tpr.	D 25	Eng.	Bulawayo, Matabeleland 1894 MMP no. 278	HC
299	Morgen, William 1890 Tpr. BSACP no. 53	Tpr.	D	C.C.	Salt River, nr. Cape Town 1896 Tpr.MMP. 1899-02 Tpr. BSAP no. 1033?	RC
309	Morris, Samuel 1893 Tpr. BBP 2023	Tpr.	B 24	Eng.	Dudley, Worcestershire 1896 Tpr. MRF	HC
495	Mostyn, Francis 1895 MMP no. 329	Tpr.	Art.	Eng.	10, Spencer Hill, Wim-bledon Lon. Severely wounded.	*Grant C.*
72	Mundell, Marmaduke Howell Gywnne 1st Ryl Dgns, 2nd L. Gds 1890 Lt. BSACP. 1893 BBP	Sgt.	G 32	Eng.	Muddeford Hse, Barnstable Devon. 1896 TSM MRF no.362 1897-1903 Lt. BSAP attached Rh. Regt. ret. 1903. D 23.2.50.	HC
293	Murphy, Daniel	Tpr.	A 23	NSW	Babranald, NSW 1895 MMP. 1896 Tpr. MRF	HC
319	Murphy, Pearce Edward 1895 MMP no. 398	Tpr.	B 34	Ire.	Balard Hse, Kilbeggan West-meath. 1896 Tpr. MRF.	HC
313	Murray, Charles Stephenson Capt. 5th Batt. Irish Rifles MMP no. 339	Tpr.	B 25	Eng.	46, Herne Hill, London 1899-02 Sgt. BSAP no. 446	HC
76	Murray, Kenneth Alexander 1893 Ptr. BBP no. 1462 1894 Sgt. MMP no. 249. 1895 MMP no. 356	Sgt.	B	SAR	Pretoria 1896 Sgt. BSAP	*Durban*
108	Musker, Edward	Cpl.	K 24	Eng.	Park C'tage, Aintree, L'pool 1896 Cpl.MRF. 1896-1905 SM BSAP 180/21	HC

u/k	Myers, Jack C. Tpr. BBP. 1894 MMP 202	Tpr.	C	Ire.	c/o JC Myers, Rathgar, Dublin Kia.	
323	Neale, Arnold Edward 1895 MMP no. 130	Tpr.	C 26	USA	Miles City, Montana 1896 Tpr. MMP. 1899-02 Tpr. BSAP no. 2422 then Pvt. no. 1084, Cape Police.	HC
321	Newitt, Henry 1890 BSACP no. 298 1894 MMP no. 165	Tpr.	B	Natal	Bulawayo, Matabeleland *Durban* 1896 Tpr. MMP. 1897 Tpr. Mt. Darwin Vols.	
322	Newman, Joseph	Tpr.	D 30	Eng.	Campbell Rd, Southsea 1896 Tpr. MRF	HC
324	Nicholls, John Edward 1890 Tpr. BSACP	Tpr.	D 32	Eng.	95, Regent St., St Helens, Ipswitch. 1896 Tpr. MRF. 1899-02 SRV. 1914-18 Rhod. Regt. OBE & Croix de Guerre	HC
325	Nicholls, Thomas Medical Staff Corps	Tpr.	B 35	Eng.	c/o Berks, Newlands, Cape Town. 1896 Tpr. MRF. 1899-1902 Spr. SRV no. 701	HC
328	Nickson, Frank A.	Tpr.	B 28	Eng.	Towcester, England Wounded. 1896 Tpr. MRF	HC
109	Normand, Patrick Hill 1893 MMP no. 109	Cpl.	A 20	Scot.	Whitehill, Aberdeen, Scot. 1899-02 Lt. ILH, DSO Gov. Fort Prison 1903. Lat. Gov. Transvaal Prison Ser. Ret. 1931 Copy Papers NAM D. 27.3.43. See WWH.	HC
326	Norris, Charles J. 1894 MMP no. 244	Tpr.	A 20	Eng.	Fox Cottage, Steering, Essex 1896 Tpr. MRF. Possibly 348 TSM Norris, BSAP D. 1.1.1900	HC
327	North, Albert	Tpr.	K 20	Eng.	Laisterdyke, Bradford, York- shire. 1896 Tpr. MRF. 1897 Tpr.RHV	HC
329	O'Dea, Thomas 1895 MMP no. 388	Tpr.	A 26	USA	198, Centre St. Boston, Mass. USA	HC
330	O'Farrell, Edward Joseph	Tpr.	C 23	Ire.	Kimberley, Griqualand W. 1896 Tpr. MMP. D. 23.4.1896	HC

49	O'Leary, John Joseph 1893 Tpr. Raaf's Col.	SM	C	C.C.	Grahamstown, C.C. 1893 SM MMP no.16. Kia 27.3.1896	RC
331	Olivers, John Redan	Tpr.	C 23	Eng.	Cape Town. 1896 Tpr. MRF	HC
332	Olsson, Gustave A.	Tpr.	A 25	Swed.	Husum, Sweden	HC
u/k	Osler, F.	Tpr.	K		Kia. Not listed on Gaberones Archive lists.	
334	Paley, John A.F.	Tpr.	G 20	Eng.	42, Stanford Place, Brighton	HC
335	Palmer, William John 1893 Tpr. BBP no. 980 1895 Tpr. MMP no. 107	Tpr.	Art. 32	Eng.	Cleveland House, Swansea 1899-1901 Tpr. BSAP no.875 1901-1902 KFS	HC
487	Palmer, James Albert 1890 BSACP	Sgt.	C	Eng.	3, Belgrave Gdns, Wands- *Illovo* worth, Lon. 1896 Sgt. MRF 1914-18 Union SA Forces	
110	Parke, William Henry Lt. 5th Batt. Connaught Rgs	Cpl.	A 25	Ire.	Cloghur Hse. Drumsun Roscommon, Ireland. 1896 Cpl. MRF	HC
111	Parker, George Bertie 1895 MMP no. 345	Cpl.	B 30	Eng.	3, Church Walk, St. Giles Oxford, England	HC
337	Parkin, Julius Minet 1895 Tpr. MMP no. 305	Tpr.	Art.	C.C.	Thorn Hill, nr. Port Elizabeth 1896 Tpr. MRF. 1898 Tpr. MMP no. 654. 1899-01 Tpr. BSAP 1092 & KTG. 1901 Tpr. WLH no. 445	RC
333	Parr, Henry, Allen Army Res. Sgt. Yorks/Lancs	Tpr.	A 29	Eng.	Mafeking, Bechuanaland 1896 Tpr.MRF. D. 17.8.96.	HC
336	Paton, Frederick William 1894 MMP no. 264	Tpr.	Art. 36	Scot.	Aberdeen 1896 Tpr. MRF	HC
353	Pattison, Reginald MMP no. 439	Tpr.	C 22	Eng.	307, Edge Lane, Liverpool Malaria	HC

352	Paul, Arthur H.D. 1895 MMP no. 360	Tpr.	Art. 20	Eng.	12, Camden Cres. Lands- down, Bath. Wounded.	HC
497	Payne, George R.	Tpr.	G	Eng.	Sea View Hse. Kingston *Inanda* by Sea, Sussex. Sly. Wounded	
338	Pechell, William Kerr 1895 MMP no. 341	Tpr.	Art. 22	Eng.	27, Great Cumberland Pl. London 1896 Tpr. MRF	HC
339	Pender, John Stuart Menzies 1893 Cpl. Vic. Col. 1893 MMP no. 54	Tpr.	B 28	Scot.	12, Hogarth Rd. London 1896 Tpr. MRF. 1896-14 TSM 541/15 & Lt. BSAP	HC
344	Pepys, Arthur Guy Leslie 1895 MMP no. 340	Tpr.	B 20	Eng.	61, Porchester Tce, London 1896 Tpr. MRF. 1897 Tpr.RHV	HC
112	Pepys, John	Cpl.	G 24	Eng.	61, Porchester Tce. Bayswater, London.	HC
341	Pescod, William Thomas	Tpr.	D 28	Eng.	Cookham Dean, Berkshire 1896 Tpr.MMP. 1899-02 Sgt. Natal Fld. Art. No.105. 1914-15 Sgt. ILH. Kia GSWA 1915.	HC
498	Philbrick, B.R.	Tpr.	A	Eng.	25 Earl Howe St Leicester *Illovo* 1896 Tpr. MMP no. 494	
340	Phillips, Francis Wall 1895 MMP 271	Tpr.	D 23	Eng.	Bulawayo, Matabeleland 1896 Tpr. MRF. 1899-1902 SSM B Sqn Rhod. Regt. no. 250 2nd ILH.	HC
342	Place, Edward Herbert 1895 MMP no. 562	Tpr.	A 23	Eng.	Skelton Grange, Yorkshire	HC
343	Plomer, Charles Campbell	Tpr.	K 25	Eng.	18, Brunswick Pl. Brighton 1896 Tpr. MRF	HC
499	Pomeroy, Granville G. 1895 MMP no. 361	Tpr.	Art.	Eng.	Leigh Woods, Clifton *Illovo* Sltly wounded 1896 Tpr. MRF	
345	Poole, Edward Josiah 1895 MMP no. 432	Tpr.	C 23	Eng.	18, Avenue Tce. Winchester 1896 Tpr. MMP	HC
500	Potter, George M. 1894 MMP no. 279	Tpr.	A	Eng.	15, Collingh Rd. West End *Illovo* Lane, Hampstead.	

u/k	Power, Patrick BBP no. 1732	Tpr.	G		Detained Pretoria by SAR. Exmember Staats Artillery. No further information.	
347	Power, Richard Edie 1895 MMP no. 424	Tpr.	B 18	Ire.	5, Garville Rd. Rathgar, Dublin. 1896 Tpr.MRF. 1897 Tpr. RHV	HC
u/k	Pownall, William Charles Beatty. MMP no. u/k	Tpr			Kia. Buried Randfontein. Incorrect. See Notes end of roll.	
346	Primmer, William Henry 1895 MMP no. 116. 1896 Tpr. MRF	Tpr.	C 25	Eng.	Vryburgh, Bechuanaland 1899-1902 Tpr. no. 254 D Sqdn. Rhod. Regt.	HC
249	Probyn, Henry	Tpr.	D 23	Eng.	Tarpoly, Cheshire 1896 Tpr. MMP	HC
238	Procter, Richard N.	Tpr.	C 31	Ire.	Salisbury, Mashonaland	HC
350	Puddy, Charles Ernest 1895 MMP no. 378	Tpr.	B 24	Eng.	Bulawayo, Matabeleland	HC
351	Pyke, George Thomas	Tpr.	G 21	Eng.	23, Stanhope Gdns, London, S.W. 1896 Tpr. MRF	HC
354	Rankins, Thomas	Tpr.	C 32	Scot.	60, Morrison St, Edinburgh 1898 SRC	HC
355	Rea, Harold George 1895 MMP no. 363	Tpr.	A 23	Eng.	1, Cranborne Tce. Richmond Surrey. 1896 Tpr. MRF	HC
74	Reeland, Charles John 1893 Tpr. BBP no. 1682	Sgt.	G 30	Eng.	Mafeking, Bechuanaland 1896 Tpr. MRF. 1899-1902 Pvt. Cape Police no. 367	HC
u/k	Reelands, W.A. BBP	Tpr.	G		Kia. Buried Doornkop. c/o P.Reelands, Forest Hse. Chingford, Essex.	
356	Reid, John Walter 1895 MMP no. 213 1896 Tpr. MRF	Tpr.	C	C.C.	Port Elizabeth 1899-1902 Cpl. E Sqn. Rhod. Regt. No. 467	RC
360	Reilby, William H. Believed Tpr. BBP no. 660	Tpr.	G	C.C.	Grahamstown	RC

358	Reynard, Joseph James D. Oct. 1937 Vic. Falls, Rhodesia	Tpr.	D	C.C.	31, Caledon St. Cape Town 1896 Tpr. Umtali Vol. Corps 1914-18 Captain	RC
357	Reynolds, Harry 1895 MMP no. 390	Tpr.	A 23	Eng.	Mawnan, Falmouth, Corn- wall. 1896 SM MRF.	HC
359	Rhodes, Charles A. 1895 MMP no. 312	Tpr.	C 28	Eng.	16, Tavistock Sq. London W.C. 1896 Tpr. MMP. 1897-1902 Sgt. BSAP no. 785. Kia 7.3.1902	HC
363	Richardson, Horace	Tpr.	C 36	Eng.	10, Palan Rd. Kingston on Thames,Surrey.1896 Tpr.MRF 1899-02 ILH. 1906 NMR	HC
364	Robert, James W. Tpr. BBP no. 1783	Tpr.	G	C.C.	Mafeking, Bechuanaland 1899-1902 Believed Tpr. II Division BSAP no.810	RC
372	Roberts, Duncan J. 1893 MMP no. 30. 1895 no. 392	Tpr.	B	C.C.	Barkley East 1896 Tpr. Mangwe Fld. Force	RC
361	Rodley, John William 1894 MMP no. 147	Tpr.	B	Eng.	Bulawayo, Matabeleland 1896 Tpr. MRF. 1897 Tpr. BSAP	HC
113	Rogers, Edward M. 1894 MMP no. 286	Cpl.	A 20	Eng.	Bichford, Perbridge, Staffs. 1896 Tpr. MRF	HC
362	Rolleston, Phillip Lancelot	Tpr.	A 25	Eng.	St. Minver, Wadebridge, Cornwall. 1896 Tpr. MRF	HC
371	Roodt, William P.	Tpr.	B	C.C.	Maitland Rd. Salt River, Cape Town.	RC
365	Rothman, John	Tpr.	D	Mash	Tuli, Matabeleland 1896 Tpr. MMP	RC
373	Rowe, Charles Frederick	Tpr.	D	C.C.	38, Constitution St. Cape Town	RC
502	Rowley, Arthur W.	Tpr.	G	C.C.	c/o Mr. RH Reynolds, *Dunn'r* Fort Peddy.	C
368	Ruck, George Gordon 1894 MMP no. 261 1895 no. 567	Tpr.	A 20	Eng.	Warlington, Surrey 1896 Tpr. MRF. no.120	HC

u/k	Ruck, Sidney Charles 1894 MMP 260	Sgt.	A		Mia. Escaped. See Pitsani Acc. Witness at Jameson's Trial. 1896 MMP no. 338	
367	Russell, Henry	Tpr.	D 27	Eng.	2, Tipnor St, Landport, Portsmouth. 1896 Tpr. MRF	HC
366	Russell, Thomas Andrew	Tpr.	G 25	Ire.	Mafeking, Bechuanaland 1896 Tpr. MRF	HC
370	Ryan, Kearns Army Reserve	Tpr.	G	Bech	Mafeking, Bechuanaland	RC
369	Ryan, Patrick Francis Army Reserve, ASC	Tpr.	C 31	Ire.	115, Barrackton, Cork.	HC
114	Rylands, Thomas E.	L/Cpl.	G 23	Eng.	Park Ho. Newport, Shropshire.	HC
375	Sainsbury, Henry	Tpr.	C 30	Eng.	Devizes, Wiltshire 1896 Tpr. MRF	HC
374	Saunders, John Drummond	Tpr.	K	C.C.	Sea Point, Cape Town 1896 Tpr. MRF	RC
377	Saunders, William G.	Tpr.	K 24	Eng.	Mafeking, Bechuanaland 1896 Tpr. MRF	HC
384	Schmeltzer, Alfred 1894 MMP no. 212	Tpr.	C	C.C.	Somerset East, C.C.	RC
378	Scott, Duncan Army Reserve	Tpr.	G 29	Scot.	Mafeking, Bechuanaland 1896 Cpl. MRF. 1897 Cpl. RHV. 1899-02 Tpr. C Sqdn Rhod. Regt. no 302	HC
115	Scrope, Gervase, J.P. 1895 MMP no. 325	Cpl.	D 22	Eng.	Danby Hall, Bredale, Yorkshire.	HC
376	Scale, George	Tpr.	G	C.C.	Port Elizabeth 1896 Tpr. MMP no. 564	RC
379	Shaw, Robert Bridge 1893-95 Tpr. MMP no.25	Tpr.	D 31	Ire.	Bulawayo, Matabeleland 1896 Tpr. MRF. 1897 Tpr. Umtali Vols.	HC

398	Shed, William Burns 1893 Tpr. Raaf's Col.	Tpr.	A 24	Scot.	Foulder, Berwick on Tweed HC Scotland. 1895 MMP no.389. 1896 Cpl. MRF
381	Sheddon, Samuel 1895 MMP no. 419	Tpr.	C 21	Scot.	Johannesburg HC
u/k	Sheppard, Henry Ainslie 1894 MMP no. 204. 1895 no. 313	Tpr.	A		Dow. 3.1.1896 Clevedon, Somerset.
388	Shoesmith, Alfred Army Res. Cpl. 2nd Y & Ls	Tpr.	K 27	Eng.	Brown's Hill, St. Helena HC
385	Sievert, Christian Henry 1894 MMP no. 183	Tpr.	B	C.C.	Kingwilliamstown C.C. RC 1896 Tpr. no. 352 A Trp. Belingwe Col. 1899-1902 SRV no. 352 Dow. Mochudi 10.3.1900
u/k	Siebert, Louis Cornelius	Tpr.	C	Swed.	Mia. Escaped. See Pitsani Acc. 1896 Tpr. No.2, BSAP
396	Simon, Louis William 1895 MMP no. 369	Tpr.	A 20	Eng.	Widmore Lge. Bromley, HC Kent. 1896 Tpr. MRF
116	Sinclair, Angus Lawrence 1890 Tpr. BSACP. 1893 Cpl. BBP no. 1573. 1894 MMP no. 171	Cpl.	Art. 30	Scot.	17, Ardconnell Tce. HC Inverness. 1896 Cpl. MRF
380	Slee, Charles Wilbourne 1893 Tpr. BBP no. 1698	Tpr.	C 27	Eng.	Bulawayo, Matabeleland HC 1896 Tpr. B Troop MMP
386	Slocock, Charles Edward	Tpr.	D 27	Eng.	Bulawayo, Matabeleland HC 1896 Tpr. MRF. 1897 Tpr. RHV. 1899-02 Sgt. SRV no. 66
117	Smith. Alexander William 1895 MMP no. 384	Cpl.	B 28	Eng.	Corton Denham, Sherborne HC Dorset. 1896 Cpl. MRF
75	Smith. Henry Walter 1893 Sgt. BBP no. 1405 1894 MMP no. 148. 1895 no. 80	Sgt.	K 34	Eng.	Mafeking, Bechuanaland HC 1896 Cpl.' L' Tpr. BFF. 1899-1902 Ord. Sgt. no.311 A Sqdn. Rhod. Regt.
383	Smith, James Joseph	Tpr.	D 27	Wales	31, Odell St. Cardiff HC 1896 Tpr. MRF

382	Smith, John Army. Res. 3rd Drgn Gds	Tpr.	K 30	Scot.	3, Hermitage Pl. Leith, Scotland. 1896 MMP	HC
390	Solomon, Percy	Tpr.	A 	C.C.	Erickville, Sea Point, Cape Town 1896 Tpr. MRF	RC
389	Spalding, Frederick William	Tpr.	G 25	Eng.	Mafeking, Bechuanaland 1896 Tpr. MRF	HC
118	Spring, Francis Raymond 1893 Tpr. BBP no. 1915 1894 MMP no. 180	Cpl.	D 27	Ire.	Bulawayo,Matabeleland 1896 Cpl. MRF. 1899-1902 Tpr. no. 525, SRV & KFS	HC
50	Springfield, Geoffrey Mandeville Osborne. 1893 Tpr. BBP no. 1447 1894 MMP no. 92	SM	D 25	Eng.	Bakousthoepe Manor, Holt, Norfolk. 1896 SM MRF 1897 Lt. BSAP	HC
395	Spurrier, D'Arce Clemence Basil Royal Horse Artillery	Tpr.	C 25	Jersey	Jersey, Channel Islands Died at sea. Typhoid fever. 6.2.1896	HC
501	Stannard, Frederick 1895 MMP no's 196/341	Tpr.	C	Eng.	134 Kennington Park, *Illovo* Park Rd. London. Stly. wounded. 1896 Tpr. MRF	
76	Stapleton, Lewis Henry 1903 Tpr. Victoria Col.	Sgt.	C 21	Eng.	31, Camden Grove, London	HC
402	Steadmond, Edward Army Reserve Royal Engineers	Tpr.	D 25	Ire.	34, Bury St. Cape Town 1896 Tpr. MRF	HC
392	Steel, Hugh 1893 Tpr. BBP no. 1402	Tpr.	Art.	Mat.	Bulawayo, Matabeleland 1894 MMP no.234. 1896 Tpr. MRF	RC
399	Steele, Alexander	Tpr.	G 30	Canada.	Mafeking, Bechuanaland 1896 Tpr. MRF	HC
404	Steer, Harry 1895 MMP no. 408	Tpr.	A 23	Eng.	4, Corporation St. Sheffield 1896 Tpr. MRF	HC
387	Steiner, Joseph Julius 1893 BBP no.1949 1894 MMP no. 128	Tpr.	Art. 29	G'man.	Bulawayo, Matabeleland 1896 Tpr. MRF. 1899-1902 Tpr. BSAP no. 2520	HC

391	Stevens, Cecil Ernest 1893 Vic. Col. 1895 MMP no. 326	Tpr.	Art.	Mat.	Bulawayo, Matabeleland 1896 Tpr. Grey's Scouts	RC
403	Stevenson, Henry 1894 MMP no. 256	Tpr.	D	C.C.	Claremont, Cape Colony	RC
u/k	Still, R.T. MMP Tpr. No. 324	Tpr.	Art.	Eng.	Dow. c/o Kenn Vicarage Somerset.	
394	Stock, Thomas Henry 1894 Tpr. BBP no.1561	Tpr.	B 35	Scot	Maryland, Dumfries, Scot. 1895 Tpr. MMP no. 382. 1896 Tpr. MRF. D. 8.10.96	HC
405	Stone (Shone) Henry John 1894 MMP no. 247	Tpr.	C	C.C.	PO Glen Byrden, Bedford Dist. Cape Colony.	RC
393	Stone, William	Tpr.	D 25	Eng.	21, George St. Upper Nor- wood, London. 1896 Tpr.MRF	HC
u/k	Stone, William B.(D) Tpr. 1155 BBP	Tpr.	K		Kia. Buried Doornkop. c/o Harry Stone, East London, CP	
119	Strutt, Charles Brownlow Lt. Irish Rifles	Cpl.	Art. 27	Eng.	Cliever Park, Windsor 1896 SM MMP, no. 310. Wia. 27.3.96. 1899-20.8.1900 Lt. BSAP. 1900 Capt. SAC.	HC
400	Sturgeon, John 1895 MMP no. 317	Tpr.	B 23	Ire.	Bulawayo, Matabeleland 1896 Tpr. MRF	HC
401	Sturton, William	Tpr.	A 31	Scot.	Ardock, Cardross, Dumbar- tonshire, Scotland.	HC
51	Sutcliffe, Herbert John 1893 Hosp. SM BBP no.1283	Hosp.SM	G	Eng. 26	Beverley, East Yorkshire	HC
397	Sutherland, Charles Edward Hartley. 1895 MMP no. 365	Tpr.	Art. 19	Eng.	19, Greencroft Gdns, South Hampstead, Lon. 1896 Cpl.MRF	HC
120	Symington, John Army Res. 3rd Drgn.Gds	Farr. Cpl.	K	Scot.	c/o Miss McMillan, Tremm- ansford, Wigton, Scotland. 1896 Cpl. MRF.	HC
77	Tapp, George Raikes 1894 MMP no. 233	Sgt.	C 25	Eng.	Blackheath, London 1896 Tpr. MRF. 1914-18 Met. Police Special Const. B.E.M. 1920. D. 21.3.51	HC

406	Taylor, Albert	Tpr.	D 22	Eng.	Cambertons Hill, Kidder-minster. 1896 Lt. MRF. Wia 21.5.96. 1899-02 Sgt. BSAP No. I Div. no.1868.	HC
u/k	Thiebert, Victor Otto MMP no. 524	Tpr.	C		Mia. Escaped. See Pitsani Acc. 1896-97 Tpr. BSAP. Cpl. SRV	
408	Thirkell, William R. 1895 MMP no.327	Tpr.	B 26	Eng.	17, Whitefriars, Hull, York-shire.	HC
407	Thomas, William Llewellyn	Tpr.	B 22	Eng.	Bulawayo, Matabeleland 1896 Cpl. Art. Troop. 1897 Cpl. RHV	HC
410	Thomson, Richard James 1893 Tpr. BBP no. 1993	Tpr.	K 23	NZ	Dunedin, New Zealand	HC
409	Thorn, Richard Adler Army Reserve	Tpr.	C 22	Eng.	6, Frome Bldg. Lwr. East-ville, Bristol. 1896 Tpr. MRF 1897 Tpr. BSAP no.495. 1899-02 SRV later ILH	HC
411	Tonge, Arthur Reginald 1895 MMP no. 126	Tpr.	C 25	Eng.	Fort Salisbury. Mashonaland 1896 Tpr. MRF	HC
u/k	Townsend				Escaped. Nothing known.	
78	Tremayne, Richard John	Sgt.	C 22	Eng.	Constantine, Penryn, Corn-wall. Eng. D. December 1942	HC
412	Turner, Arthur Francis Bowley. 1894 MMP no. 214	Tpr.	B	Natal	c/o Mrs CR Turner, *Durban* Pretoria, SAR. 1896 Tpr. MMP, BSAP no's. 1675/367.	
413	Tytleton, George H.	Tpr.	D	C.C.	Mowbray, Cape Town	RC
u/k	Valle B.W. (Leon)(Valeriani) 1890. Tpr. 334 BSACP	Tpr.	A		Mia. Escaped. See Pitsani Acc. 1894 Tpr. MMP 414. See Notes end of Roll.	
414	Vanner, Clement William 1893 Tpr. BBP no.1111	Tpr.	C	C.C.	North Battery, Simonstown 1896 Tpr. MMP	RC
415	Victor, Arthur 1893 Gifford's Horse	Tpr.	Art.	Mat.	Bulawayo, Matabeleland 1894 Cpl. MMP no. 248 1895 MMP no. 294	RC

418	Wagstaff, St.John Henry 1893 TSM BBP no. 1250 1894 MMP no. 181	Tpr.	Art. 28	Eng.	110, Tressillion Rd. St. John's, London, SE. 1897 MMP no. 648 1899-1902 Tpr. BSAP no. 480	HC
419	Waites, Joseph 1895 MMP no. 416	Tpr.	A	SAR	c/o Mrs Waites, Harrison *Durban* St. Jo'burg. 1897-8 MMP No. 653. 1896 Tpr. A Troop, Belingwe Column.	
417	Walker, Fred. V. Poss. Felix Vaughan	Tpr.	D 28	Eng.	Salt River, nr. Cape Town 1896 Tpr. BSAP	HC
420	Walker, Thomas J.	Tpr.	G 33	Eng.	Oldbury Works, Tewkes- bury, Gloucestershire. 1896 Gnr. BFF. 1899-1902 Tpr. BSAP 1176 (1172?)	HC
121	Wallace/Wallis, Harry	Cpl.	K 26	Eng.	50, Forest Rd,West Notting- ham. 1896 Tpr. no.102 Mangwe F.F. 1899-1900 Lt. BSAP. D. 21.4.1900	HC
416	Walters, Albert Edward	Tpr.	D 21	Eng.	Somerville, Willesdon Lane, London. 1896 Tpr. MMP	HC
421	Walterstorff, Albert Johann. 1895 MMP no. 409	Tpr.	B 28	Swed.	Stockholm. 1896 MRF. 1897 Mt. Darwin Vols. 1898-1924 Cpl. BSAP nos. 789 & 56.	HC
423	Weare, Robert Augustus	Tpr.	K	C.C.	Grahamstown.	RC
425	Webb, Benjamin William 1894 MMP no. 287	Tpr.	Art. 35	Eng.	Graaf Reinet, C.C. 1896 Sgt. MRF. 1897 MMP no.632. 1899-02 Tpr. no.6 C in C BG & CTTG (SM). Pte. Cape Infantry.	HC
422	Webb, Churchland J.	Tpr.	A 21	Eng.	Eathorpe, Leamington Spa, Warwickshire.1896 Tpr.MRF	HC
424	Wedderburn, John	Tpr.	D 28	Eng.	Newcastle on Tyne 1896 Tpr. MRF.	HC
434	Weldon, Henry 1895 MMP no. 128	Tpr.	C	C.C.	Port Elizabeth	RC

u/k	Weinthal, Paul 1893 Tpr. Victoria Col.	Tpr.	A		Mia. Escaped. 1893 MMP no. 76. 1896 Tpr. MRF	
427	Wenn, Edmund W.	Tpr.	G 27	Eng.	Tretasler Villa, Launceston Cornwall. 1896 Tpr. MRF	HC
426	Wetherall, George John 1894 MMP no. 258	Tpr.	B 21	Eng.	Bulawayo, Matabeleland 1896 Tpr. MRF. 1899-02 Tpr. BSAP no. 876	HC
122	White, George James Army Reserve	Cpl.	G 29	Tasman.	10, Hartland Rd,CamdenTn. London. 1896 Tpr. MRF. 1899-02 Tpr. BSAP no. 2402	HC
430	Wickham, Thomas Strange 1895 MMP no. 330	.Tpr.	Art. 19	Eng.	Bideford, Devon. 1896 Tpr. MRF	HC
431	Wiggins, Thomas Army Res. Pte. 3rd Drgn Gds	Tpr.	K 28	Eng.	149, High St. Fulham, London.	HC
u/k	Wiley, Harry MMP no. 413	Tpr.	B		Mia. Escaped. Reported Byo. Chronicle. See Pitsani Account. 1896 Sgt. Belingwe Column.	
u/k	Willan, Frederick (T) 1893 Tpr. Vic. Col. MMP no. 63	Tpr.	D		Mia. Escaped. 1895 MMP no. 250. 1896 Tpr. MRF.	
435	Willam, Albert C.	Tpr.	B	SAR	Johannesburg. *Durban*	
u/k	Williams, J.W (T.W) MMP no. 402	Tpr.	B		Mia. Escaped.	
123	Williamson, John James 1896 MMP no.1. D. 26.1.97	Cpl.	G 28	Ire.	Braff, Kilmillock, Limerick Ireland. 1896 Sgt. MRF	HC
52	Willows, Tom Oxden 1893 TSM BBP. no. 887	Trp.SM	K	C.C.	Grahamstown, C.C. 1895 MMP no.182. 1896 SM MRF	RC
428	Wilmot, George Rates 1895 MMP no. 429	Tpr.	A	C.C.	Grahamstown	RC
432	Wilmot, William McDonald.	Tpr.	B	C.C.	Grahamstown	RC
	1895 MMP no. 430					
433	Wilson, David Army Res. Pte. 3rd Drgn Gds	Tpr.	K 30	Scot.	Mafeking, Bechuanaland	HC

503	Wilson, John 1893 Raaf's Col. MMP no.28	Tpr.	C	Eng.	33, Oval R. Hastings Rd. *Illovo* London. 1896 Tpr. MRF
79	Winder, Allan Campbell	Sgt.	D 25	Ire.	Lourville, Rathfarnham, Co. HC Dublin, Ire. 1896 Sgt. MRF. 1897 MMP no.103. 1899-00 Rhod. Regt. Kia Crocodile 13.2.1900
429	Wintle, George Stanley	Tpr.	A 22	Eng.	9, Grantham Villas, Oxford HC 1896 Tpr. MRF. 1899-1901 Cpl. Rimmington's Scts. 1901-02 Lt. WPMR D. August, 1952.
u/k	Wiid, Paul Stewart Cape Garrison Artillery	Tpr.	C		Believed Dow. Krugersdorp. See Pitsani Acc. c/o Mrs Wiid, Litchfield Cottage, Woodstock.
436	Young, Anthony Rogers	Tpr.	K 25	Eng.	Mafeking, Bechunaland. HC 1896 Tpr. MRF
437	Zeiss, Edward Charles A. 1893 Tpr. BBP no. 1854	Tpr.	G	C.C.	Kimberley RC
440	Basson, Albertus J.	Noncomb't		C.C.	Lower Paarl, C.C. RC
439	Blasson, George H.	Noncomb't		SAR	Johannesburg, SAR *Durban* 1896 Tpr. BSAP no. 679
443	Garlick, Burleigh 1893 Tpr. Vic. Column.	Noncomb't		--	Dr. Jameson's servant. *Victoria*
441	McDonnell, John	Noncomb't		Eng.	78, St. Lawry Rd. Cape T. HC 1896 Tpr. MRF. 1899-02 Tpr. BSAP no. 851
438	Pettit, George E.	Noncomb't		Eng.	c/o PO Colchester, Essex HC Lt. Grenfell's servant
442	Woodruff, Frederick G.	Noncomb't		Eng.	North Hill, Colchester. HC

NOTES:

Beatty, William Charles Pownall — This is an error so must be listed unknown. The subject was killed by accidental gun discharge in April, 1896 while serving in the Belingwe Laager during the Matabele Rebellion. See Matabele Rebellion by Major Tyrie Laing.

Valle. — MMP no. 670 is listed as Burton William Valley, possibly another person

HARLECH CASTLE

DRIVERS, LEADERS, CARRIERS, SERVANTS, etc.

444	John Nel	Cape man	Harrismith, OFS	*Natal*
445	John Price	"	Cape Town	"
446	David	"	Paarl, Cape Colony	"
447	Albert	"	Paarl, C.C.	"
448	John Isaacs	"	Somerset West	"
449	Kus Meyer	"	Graaf Reinet	"
450	Abraham Williams	"	Wynberg, C.C.	"
451	Gert Friesland	"	Port Elizabeth	"
452	Charles Cornelius	"	Kimberley	"
453	John Cornelius	"	Kimberley	"
454	Peter Booysen	"	Kimberley	"
455	Majackajack	Native	Sunday's River, Ladysmith	"
456	August Nel	Mashona	Bulawayo	"
457	William Buss	Griqua	Bloemfontein, OFS	"
458	Tom Seaman	Native Mozambique	Grahamstown, C.C.	"
459	Stoffel Booysen	Basuto	Mafeking, Bechuanaland	"
460	Andrew Innes	Cape man	Craddock, C.C.	"
461	Jaffie Jacobs	Basuto	Mafeking, Bechuanaland	"
462	Jack Koodoo	Native Natal	Pietermaritzburg, Natal	"
463	Malbaya or Mabraza	Native	Sterkstroom, Queenstown, C.C.	"
464	Phillip Fouchie	Mean White	Kimberley, C.C.	"
465	John Pritchard	Bastard	Cape Town	"
466	Harry Brown	Bastard	Port Elizabeth	"
467	Tom	Native Natal	Polela Div. Natal	"
468	Jack	Bastard	Mafeking, Bechuanaland	"
469	Jack	Native	Mafeking, Bechuanaland	"
470	Frog	Basuto	Jona Kraus country, Basutoland	"
471	Whisky	Native	Inhambane, PEA	"
472	Joseph	Native	Breakfeast Vlei, Grahamstown, C.C.	"
473	Dick	Native	Bechuanaland	"
474	Joe	Matabele	Bulawayo, Matabeleland	"
475	Tom Dubuys	Cape man	Mafeking, Bechuanaland	"
476	Martinus Botha	Cape man	Mafeking, Bechuanaland	"
477	Piccanninni	Native	Bamangwato, Khama's country	"
478	Klein John	Native	Mafeking, Bechuanaland	"
479	Jim Mashona	Native	Salisbury, Mashonaland	"
480	Bushman	Bushman	Bulawayo, Matabeleland	"
481	Fryingpan	Native	Bulawayo, Matabeleland	"
482	Kleinbooi	Native	Sibele's tribe, Bechuanaland	"
483	Babajan	Native	Bulawayo, Matabeleland	"
484	Daniel	Native	Mafeking, Bechuanaland	"

NOTE ON THE ANGLO-BOER WAR, 1899 – 1902

While it is perhaps too much to say that the Jameson Raid was a major cause of the Anglo-Boer War it was certainly a contributing factor. The Raid solidified in the mind of the Transvaal Government that designs were being made on their territory and sovereignty.

It is therefore fitting to give a very brief note to the participation in this War of the British South Africa Police and none more fitting to write it than A.J. Tomlinson who was on active service in it.

A.J. Tomlinson joined the Bechuanaland Border Police in 1893. In October, 1894, he transferred to the Mashonaland Mounted Police and was commissioned as a Sub-Inspector/Lieutenant in 1895. He took part in the Jameson Raid and was sent to England with the other prisoners but soon returned and was a member of the Matabele Relief Force during the Matabele Rebellion. In 1899 he went with the B.S.A.P. Detachment to the South African War and was promoted Captain during this period of service.

After the War he resumed his career in the B.S.A.P. and in 1916 he was appointed first Officer Commanding of the Rhodesia Native Regiment and served with it in the German East Africa campaign in World War One. In 1926 he was appointed Acting Commissioner of the B.S.A.P.

He also wrote valuable accounts of service with the Rhodesia Native Regiment and the Anglo-Boer War.

The following article was published in the December, 1941, issue of *The Outpost*.

B.S.A. Police Squadron on parade at Bulawayo prior to
departure for active service, 1900.

SOUTH AFRICAN WAR

By: Lieut.-Col. A.J. Tomlinson

This is a brief narrative of the part taken by the B.S.A. Police in the South African War – 1899-1902.

Soon after the outbreak of hostilities in 1899, Capt. Hoel Llewellyn was sent in an armoured train with a maxim gun and a detachment of the B.S.A. Police into Bechuanaland: this was the means of preventing the Boers from advancing beyond Gaberones; further detachments were sent by train to the South as operations increased.

Col. Plumer commanded the forces from Southern Rhodesia, and there were several engagements with the enemy in which the B.S.A. Police took part; finally Plumer formed a military camp at Sefetili (Bechuanaland) in April, 1900, to await an opportune time to relieve Mafeking, which was being heavily attacked. With Plumer's troops were three squadrons of B.S.A. Police under Capt. Bowden (with Lieuts. Bateson and McGee), Capt. Nesbitt, V.C. (with Lieuts. Moore and Howes), and Lieut. Tomlinson (with Lieuts. Wood and Godley), the whole commanded by Lieut.-Col. Bodle.

(Note: Regarding Lieut. Tomlinson commanding a Squadron, there was no 'Acting Captain' rank in those days.)

Inspecting an armoured train at Bulawayo.

In the group are (L to R) Col. Nicholson, Col. Baden-Powell, Capt. Lllewellyn and Railway Engineer Mr. Wallis.

On 15 May, 1900, Plumer started with his whole column for Mafeking, meeting on the way a column from the South under Col. Mahon. It is well-known that the combined forces were victorious, and the enemy was defeated after somewhat severe fighting and Mafeking was relieved on 17 May, 1900.

No time was then wasted, and the B.S.A. Police, under Col. Bodle, were soon on the march into the Transvaal, making for Rustenburg, where operations were conducted for some time in the district; the B.S.A. Police were allotted positions on the hills surrounding the town, and it was not long before fighting took place with a Boer commando from the South; this was driven off, and a fierce fight took place soon afterwards at Warmbaths, whence Plumer's forces pursued another commando, which was repulsed and which then retired.

A part of Plumer's troops at Rustenburg consisted of an Australian regiment which, whilst on patrol one day, was trapped in a hilly pass some thirty miles from the town. When the news came in, the B.S.A. Police, under Col. Bodle, were immediately detailed to go to the 'Aussies' assistance. With the arrival of this force, the enemy retired, but had inflicted a loss of nineteen killed and many wounded of the Australians, with a number of horses captured, before the B.S.A. Police got to the Pass.

And so it went on from day to day, fighting when the enemy was encountered.

As the Rustenburg district became fairly quiet, Col. Plumer's force moved towards Pretoria and took up a position near the M'silikatzi Pass in the Magaliesburg Range. Here the B.S.A. Police were sent, with other detachments in turn, on daily patrols; guerrilla warfare was now the order of the day in the surrounding country.

Some time elapsed and then news came through that Pretoria had been taken by Lord Roberts on 4 June, whereupon the B.S.A. Police, with the rest of Plumer's column, marched to the Transvaal capital and were camped just outside the town.

Although it was considered that the Boers would now give in altogether, it was soon found that they intended to carry on with guerrilla tactics, so 120 B.S.A. Police (under Major Hanbury Tracey) were again sent to Rustenburg. Shortly after, the garrison was surrounded by a superior enemy force, and but for the timely arrival of reinforcements of a detachment of an Imperial regiment, would undoubtedly have had to capitulate.

On another occasion the Australian regiment on patrol was again surrounded near a place called Eland's River, when 39 men were killed or wounded, and many horses shot or stampeded, and but for Capt. FitzClarence with the Protectorate regiment and a detachment of B.S.A. Police coming to the rescue, our force must have surrendered.

The B.S.A. Police took part in various minor operations at this time, and eventually were released from service and returned to Southern Rhodesia in December, 1900.

But the anticipated conclusion of hostilities did not come about, and so, on 27 September, 1901, Major Drury, with Lieuts. Chapman and Ingham, with 125 N.C.O.s and men, left Bulawayo for Mafeking and joined Lord Methuen's column; a further 25 men under Lieut. Agar were also sent South in February, 1902.

An unfortunate occurrence happened when a British convoy of Lord Methuen's column was captured in February, 1902. The detachment of B.S.A. Police, under Lieut. Ingham, was escort to the guns on this occasion and fought for nearly three hours, and did not surrender until completely surrounded. The officer in charge of the guns afterwards wrote to Col. Bodle in high terms of the gallantry of the B.S.A. Police.

Major Drury's detachment of the B.S.A. Police continued with the Imperial troops until the conclusion of the war in May, 1902.

The foregoing is merely an outline of the services rendered by the B.S.A. Police in the South African War. **It should be placed on record that His Majesty King Edward VII was pleased to mark his appreciation of the services of the B.S.A. Police by the presentation of colours to the Corps, which are valued exceedingly.**

ADDITIONAL SUMMARY.

The British South Africa Police were engaged on active service in the South African War from 1899 to 1902.

Before the outbreak of war a force had been mobilised at Tuli under the command of Lieut.-Col. Bodle, and upon the commencement of hostilities on 11 October, 1899, was attached to Col. Plumer's column. Two-thirds of this detachment came from the Matabeleland division of the Police, and the remainder, under Capt. R. Nesbitt, V.C., was drawn from the Mashonaland division.

After the cessation of fighting in the region of Tuli and Rhodes Drift, the B.S.A. Police went with Col. Plumer's main forces to Mochudi via Palapye, and took part in many engagements in which a number of casualties were sustained. It is recorded that Lieut.-Col. Bodle was in command of the advance guard prior to the relief of Mafeking. Col. Plumer's forces at this time included three squadrons of B.S.A. Police. In addition to these operations, Capt. Hoel Llewellyn was in charge of a detachment of Police who manned the armoured trains. At this time the Boers were doing much damage to the railway line between Mafeking and Gaberones. Col. Plumer in his report states that the reason the damage done was not more extensive, and was not allowed to spread further North, was due to a great extent to the armoured trains organised by Col. J. Nicholson, D.S.O., Commandant-General of the B.S.A.P., and commanded by Capt. Llewellyn.

Capt. Bowden, in charge of a small force, was sent to Magalapye to assist the Protectorate chief Khama in case of attack, and a force including some 108 B.S.A.P., under the command of Col. Holdsworth, assisted by Capt. G.V. Drury, moved South, repairing the railway line as they advanced.

Following the relief of Mafeking, Lieut.-Col. Bodle's column accompanied Col. Plumer's and General Baden-Powell's forces into the Transvaal, and the B.S.A. Police detachment captured Boer guns at Rustenburg. Until the arrival of the Canadian contingent in May, 1900, the only artillery available to Col. Plumer was that supplied by the B.S.A. Police.

On the resumption of regular duties by the B.S.A. Police, the following telegram, dated 19 November, 1900, from the Military Secretary, Chief Army Headquarters, Johannesburg, addressed to Col. Bodle, British South Africa Police, Bulawayo, was received:-

> The British South Africa Police, having left Pretoria to return to their regular duties, the Field Marshal Commander-in-Chief desires to place on record his high appreciation of the admirable work done by the Corps throughout the campaign. Lord Roberts much regrets he was unable to see the British South Africa Police before they left his command, and requests that you will accept yourself and convey to officers, non-commissioned officers and men, how much he valued the gallant service they have rendered during the past year of hard work, hard fighting and scanty fare.

In September, 1901, the B.S.A.P. were again on active service. At the request of Lord Methuen, Col. Bodle, with Capt. (later Major) G.V. Drury and a force of some 130 men, left Bulawayo for Mafeking, and in February, 1902, were reinforced at Vryburg by a further smaller detachment. This force was in action at Driefontein, when they fought a rearguard action to the

Yeomanry, in the course of which they lost two policemen killed and five wounded. At Klerksdorp, on 25 February, one N.C.O. and two men were seriously wounded, and in Lord Methuen's engagement on 7 March, four men were killed and a number of casualties incurred. The detachment was publicly thanked by Lord Methuen at Lichtenburg for conspicuous service in this campaign.

Maxim Gun Company of Australian and New Zealand Imperial Bushmen accompanying Plumer's last advance to join up with Mahon

ON BRITISH SOUTH AFRICA POLICE

BANNERS, BATTLE HONOURS AND

MEMORIALS

CLIFF ROGERS (4735)

THE BANNER VERSUS COLOUR

CONTROVERSY

Banner or Colour – the cause of the controversy

THE B.S.A.P. BANNER

The saga of the B.S.A.P. Banner has been around for a long time and I do not think that this article will provide all the answers required. The 'Banner' was one of seventy-one that were awarded on the instructions of the then king, Edward VII, to units that had served in the Anglo-Boer War and who did not have a Regimental or Sovereign's Colour. At the time it was stated that they were not to be used or designated as a regimental colour and that 'Battle Honours' were not to be emblazoned on the banner. (*See the copy of the original authorisation.*) Many of the units named who received a banner subsequently ignored these instructions, instances abound where banners were used as a colour and battle honours embroidered thereon. Also as footnote I believe the banners were supplied as a plain Union flag and the regimental badges emblazoned thereon were at the regiment's expense.

Historically a Sovereign's Colour was awarded to a regiment by the sovereign of the day and would be renewed periodically. The Regimental Colour was not issued by the Sovereign, in the past when the government or the sovereign of the day ordered a new regiment to be formed it was the custom for the ladies of the regiment to get together and make a distinctive regimental colour. In the days of high illiteracy the men needed an identifiable point on which to rally in battle. There was no need to seek permission, it was a natural sequence that this task would be undertaken and a colour provided. Later in history this ad hoc system was changed and the design had to be approved by the Inspector of Regimental Colours. As Colonel Tim Wright mentions in an article on the Northern Rhodesia Police, the N.R.P. had a King's Colour but no Regimental Colour until July, 1924, when they were handed a Regimental Colour which was the gift of the European Ladies of the Territory. This colour was made by the Royal School of Needlework in London and approved by the Inspector of Regimental Colours.

The office of Inspector of Regimental Colours was instituted in 1806 in order to regulate the design of the various Colours, Guidons and Standards of the Army. Regulations for these had been laid down in 1768 but these regulations were widely ignored and designs left to the wishes of individual colonels. The first Inspector was George Nayler (1764 – 1831), York Herald, later Garter King of Arms. As the Army's heraldic adviser he is responsible for approving all new designs for Colours, Guidons, Standards, Cap Badges, Defence Agencies, etc. The artwork for all new designs is prepared at the

College of Arms by a heraldic artist, signed by the Inspector and then submitted to the Queen, via the Ministry of Defence, for formal approval. Once the Queen has signed the painting it is returned to the College for safe keeping.

I would hazard a guess that at its inauguration in 1896 and afterwards, that if anyone had pushed hard enough the Regiment of Mounted Infantry known as the British South Africa Police could have acquired a Regimental Colour.

However, back to the 'Banner.' Obviously over the years this was treated as and thought of as a 'Colour.' The problem arose when the banner needed a replacement and it became apparent that the B.S.A.P. was not entitled to a colour and that there would be no replacement. The story developed over the years and is poorly documented. (*See the efforts to resolve this saga documented on Page 5 by an unknown author.*) I received this memorandum many years ago via Mike Leach, the then Secretary of the United Kingdom Branch of the Regimental Association, and I trust if the author recognises his work he will accept my thanks. Also relevant is a copy of an email I received many years ago from the late Alan Rich who had also endeavoured to fill the gaps.

I might also add a quotation I came across while researching this material which I feel is very apt.

> A moth-eaten rag on a worm-eaten pole,
> It does not look likely to stir a man's Sole,
> 'Tis the deeds that were done 'neath the moth-eaten rag,
> When the pole was a staff and the rag was a flag.

(Sir Edward Hamly on seeing some old Colours of the 32nd Foot in Monmouth Church.)

CONFIDENTIAL.
South Africa.
No. 9249.
From Field-Marshal Lord Roberts to the Adjutant-General. Received 13th
November, 10.33 p.m.)
(Telegram.)
(No. 1513, code.) Johannesburg, 13th November 1900, 12.45 p.m.

Following is complete list of all Colonial corps who desire to send
detachments to England with their correct designations:—

Royal Canadian Artillery, Royal Canadian Dragoons, Royal Canadian
   Regiment, Royal Canadian Mounted Rifles, Lord Strathcona's Horse.
   Total, Canadian, 5 banners.

Lumsden's Horse. India, 1 banner.

Ceylon — Ceylon Mounted Infantry. Ceylon, 1 banner.

New Zealand Bushmen, New Zealand Mounted Rifles.
   Total. New Zealand, 2 banners.

Tasmanian Bushmen, Tasmanian Mounted Rifles.
   Total. Tasmania, 2 banners.

New South Wales Artillery, New South Wales Lancers, Australian Horse,
   New South Wales Mounted Rifles, New South Wales Bushmen, New
   South Wales Medical Staff Corps.
   Total, New South Wales, 6 banners.

South Australia, Victoria, Queensland, and West Australia, each 2 corps,
   Mounted Rifles and Bushmen.
   Total for these 4 Colonies, 8 banners.

Cape Colony Corps. — Commander-in-Chiefs Bodyguard, Border Horse,
   Border Scouts, Brabant's Horse, Prince Alfred's Own Cape Artillery,
   Prince Alfred's Own Cape Garrison Artillery, Cape Mounted Rifles, Cape
   Police, Cape Town Highlanders, Cape Volunteer Medical Staff Corps,
   Duke of Edinburgh's Own Volunteer Rifles, Eastern Province Horse,
   First City (Grahamstown) Volunteers, Kaffrarian Rifles, Kimberley
   Regiment, Kitchener's Horse, Loch's Horse, Marshall's Horse, Nesbitt's
   Horse, Orpen's Horse, Prince Alfred's Own Volunteer Guard,
   Queenstown Rifle Volunteers, Railway Pioneer Regiment, Roberts's
   Horse, South African Light Horse, Uitenhage Volunteer Rifles.
   Total, Cape Colony, 21 banners.

Natal Corps — Bethune's Mounted Infantry, Border Mounted Rifles,
Durban Light Infantry, Imperial Light Horse, Imperial Light Infantry,
Natal Carbineers, Natal Field Artillery, Natal Mounted Rifles, Natal
Naval Volunteers, Natal Volunteer Medical Staff, Natal Police,
Thorneycroft's Mounted Infantry, Umvoti Mounted Rifles.
Total, Natal, 15 banners.

Rhodesian and other corps — Bechuanaland Rifles, British South Africa
Police, Protectorate Regiment, Rhodesian Regiment, Southern
Rhodesian Volunteers.
Total Rhodesian, 5 banners.

Grand total, 71 banners.

It is possible that several of these corps may not send representatives when
the time arrives, but all have applied to do so.

SUMMARY OF A FILE DEALING WITH THE B.S.A.P. BANNER, RECENTLY LOCATED IN THE NATIONAL ARCHIVES IN HARARE, ZIMBABWE

On 17 October, 1922, the B.S.A.P. held a 'Board' into the dilapidated state of the King's Colour of the B.S.A.P. The members of the Board were Majors Ingham and Dacomb and Lt. Bugler.

As a result of their deliberations the Administrator, Drummond Chaplin, wrote to the Earl of Connaught, High Commissioner for South Africa, in Pretoria asking that the King's Colour, presented to the B.S.A.P. in May, 1904, be replaced. It was mentioned that this was one of 64 presented to permanent Colonial units taking part in the South African War and was referred to in a Dispatch of Lord Milner (1011 of 14.11.1904), then High Commissioner for South Africa, on behalf of King Edward VII. (It was also a recommendation that the unsuitable Colour be lodged in the Cathedral for safe-keeping.)

(Note by HCP. The reader will doubtless have spotted that the 'flag' has already been variously referred to as a 'banner' and a 'colour', also that there is an apparent discrepancy in dates.)

On 1 May, 1923, it was intimated that as no duplicate could be obtained (Army funds cannot meet a replacement) the Banner could be replaced by a silk Union Flag similar, but not identical, to that originally presented. This offer was accepted and the substitute dispatched from the Barrack stores in Pimlico to the B.S.A. Coy. in Pretoria during June of that year.

In mid-1926, Dacomb indicated via the 'correct channels' that the B.S.A.P. required Regimental Colours and was advised on 16 October, 1926, that 'there is no record in the Dominions Office of authority for the B.S.A.P. to carry a Regimental Colour.

Soon after this, in September, 1928, the Royal School of Needlework came into the act. Following a letter saying that in December, 1924, they had repaired the King's Service Colour for £14 13s 3p, they intimated that IF (my capitals) the B.S.A.P. had been granted permission by the King to have a Colour, then the Regiment should submit appropriate and historically correct designs. If permission had NOT been granted then an approach should be made to His Majesty through the Colonial Office.

(Note by HCP. I suggest that there is a letter missing in all this and that reference to the Royal School MIGHT disclose something although, in the long run, it makes not an iota of difference.)

The story now moves on some years – probably in the run-up to the Coronation in 1937 – when once more Ingham appears on the scene, saying that the B.S.A.P. were given Regimental Colours for service in the Boer War and that Bodle was in charge of the Colour Party from Bulawayo, that the group included S.M. Chalmers, Sergeant Cockerham and himself with four others and that Colours were also presented to the Southern Rhodesia Volunteers (Matabeleland).

There is a partial summation that the Banner was given in recognition of services rendered to the Empire. It was NOT a Colour and by command of His Majesty, the late King Edward VII, battle honours were NOT allowed to be emblazoned on it.

In March, 1937, comment is made that no record exists in the War Office or the Dominions Office of the granting of permission to the B.S.A.P. to carry colours.

I suppose, looking through all this again, that many of those involved in the saga just did not know the difference between a Banner, a King's Colour, Regimental Colours and a handkerchief! This puts them exactly in the same position as myself! What does seem reasonably certain is that the B.S.A.P. never had 'Colours' in the military sense, certainly could never put Battle Honours on if they possessed one. This is academic as at this time they did not have a battle honour. It would be of interest to know what happened to the banner and its successors.

EMAIL FROM ALAN RICH (4547)

Subject: BSAP Battle Honours
Date: Wed, 6 Sep 2000 15:42:05 +0200
From: "A.W.Rich"

Dear Al,

Had a spare 15 minutes this morning at the Archives where I dropped off some Law Books not suitable for the Police Museum and caught sight of a card headed BSAP Colours - drew the file and here follows very much a precis as did not have pencil with me and as you know pens are verbotten.

Appears that in about 1923 the original Banner presented in 1904 had become very threadbare and Compol via the High Commissioner had writted to Dominion Office requesting that a replacement "Colour" be supplied.

Quite some correspondence ensued including a letter to some Nunnery in England, who replied that they would be willing to embroider the Flag provided they had proof that the BSAP were entitled to have same.

Meanwhile correspondence between High Commissioner and Dominion Office continued and eventually there appeared the final letter - I scribbled down the bulk and it reads

"Dominion Office advise that the Flag presented to BSAP on 1904 was not a Colour and Battle Honours were not allowed to be emblazoned on it. There is no record in the War Office or the Dominion Office of granting of permission to BSAP to carry Colours"

It does appear that another similar item to the original Banner was supplied from South Africa or Army sources (will have to properly check this bit) and the original given to Salisbury Cathedral for "hanging" therein. So the one which was in the Officers' Mess from about 1928 was a duplicate.

I also checked the Regimental (Force) Orders for 1925 - only the period Jan to June is present and that in a hand written ledger. No trace of any suggestion that the BSAP were awarded battle honours.

Now I agree that the comments re the Flag and Banner do not absolutely refute/support the suggestion that the BSAP were ever granted Battle Honours but it does seem that they were not so given is the more plausible explanation.

I will, time and petrol permitting (lazy so and so, easy walking distance!!) draw the Banner/Flag papers and prepare a full article for the ZMS Journal and may put it on the BSAP email system, if the finished item appears suitable.

One other item of note, especially for Geoff , although he maybe aware of the fact that there is a card under BSAP 1890-1898 which reads ":High Commissioner for South Africa. Ref S1428/8 - this file retained in Botswana" and goes on to say S1428/7 - Part held in Harare Archives.

There are about 40 cards all under BSAP covering medals, nominal rolls, crime reports and so on, will take ages to go through them all, but in October I should be getting a laptop from UK, via SA and that will reduce the time spent trying to decipher my hand written scrawl. Peter - there is definitely NOT one marked Sherwood-Kelly or any permutation of the name!!

All for today, toodle pip Chaps.

Alan.

110

From: Major D Rankin-Hunt MVO TD

NORFOLK HERALD OF ARMS EXTRAORDINARY

28th November 2000

Dear Mr Rogers,

I am replying to your letter of the 1st November regarding the British South Africa Police.

Regrettably there is nothing in the College records which would shed any light on this subject. It would appear therefore, that if any Banners were presented they would have been approved in that country.

Yours sincerely,

Daniel Rankin Hunt

Deputy Inspector of Regimental Colours

C.E. Rogers Esq.,
20 Home Way,
Petersfield,
Hampshire GU31 4EE

7 Cumberland Lodge Mews, The Great Park, Windsor, Berkshire SL4 2JD Tel: 01784 437269

BATTLE HONOURS

The British South Africa Police did not receive a battle honour for their service in the Anglo-Boer War, however, there are numerous references that show why an honour was denied.

The Regiment felt badly treated in the matter and although the case was made for an honour to be granted the files show that it went to the top and was rejected.

There is no doubt that a 'Battle Honour' was earned but the regulations of the time did not allow the B.S.A.P. to receive one as the B.S.A.P. did not operate as a complete unit. The rule being that a unit had to operate with at least 50% of their strength and their own H.Q. Staff to qualify. There is a letter written by Colonel Bodle that makes the case for an honour. In the letter he points out that at one period during the war the Regiment had 835 officers & men under arms in the field for over a period of one year. In comparison, many units with a fraction of these numbers were granted the honour 'South Africa 1900'. In the Regiment's case the rules do seem to have been harshly interpreted. One composite unit formed by the three Household Cavalry Regiments existed where none of the above conditions were met and yet each individual regiment was granted a battle honour after the war and bears it proudly on their colour. A comparison of unit strength and length of service in the theatre shows:-

1st Lifeguards.   1 Sqn. 268 Officers & men. Dec. 1899 - Nov. 1900.
2nd Lifeguards.   1 Sqn. 249 Officers & men, Dec. 1899 - Nov. 1900.
1st Royal Horseguards. 1 Sqn. 292 Officers & men. Dec. 1899 - Nov. 1900.
                   Battle Honours. 'Relief of Kimberley', 'Paardeberg' & 'South Africa 1899-1900'.
Leicestershire Yeomanry. Sponsored 2 Companies I.Y. Approx. 200 Officers & men.
                   Battle Honour. 'South Africa 1900 – 1902'.
B.S.A.P.   **1792 Officers & men. Oct.1899 – May 1902.**

The 3rd Wiltshires Regiment & the 4th Gloucestershire Regiment received the honour 'St. Helena' for guarding prisoners of war on that island.

Yeomanry Regiments that had provided more than 20 men to the local Imperial Yeomanry Company could also be granted the honour. It is difficult to discover the reason for this refusal. Possibly if the B.S.A.P. had

had a Royal as Colonel in Chief or a couple of senior officers in the War Office who had regimental connections things might have been different.

This article does not infer that the above Regiments should not have received these honours only to argue for the case that the B.S.A.P. also deserved the honour for their service.

However the Regiment did receive the honour 'E.Africa 1915-18' for their services in World War I. This was allowed as they fought in that conflict as a complete unit of battalion strength. This is confirmed by a document submitted to and signed by King George V on the 4th May 1925.

The Rhodesian units mentioned in the document were:-

1. The British South Africa Police.
   The Great War - 1 Battalion.
   'E. Africa 1915-18'.
2. The 1st Rhodesia Regiment.
   The Great War - 1 Battalion.
   'S.W. Africa 1914-15'.
3. The 2nd Rhodesia Regiment,
   The Great War - 1 Battalion.
   'Kilimanjaro', 'Behobebo' 'E. Africa 1915-17'.
4. The 1st Rhodesia Native Regiment.
   The Great War - 1 Battalion.
   'East Africa 1916-18'.
5. The 2nd Rhodesia Native Regiment.
   The Great War – 1 Battalion.
   'E. Africa 1917-18'.

See copies of documents used in the meeting to review the request for the battle honour. The documents were found in the WO32 and the CO417 Series at The National Archives, Kew. They support what we already know. Note KGV's initials on the WW One document (page 105).

REGISTER No. 079   **Minute Sheet No. 6**

General rules hitherto observed.

2.

The general rules governing the grant of South African honours, as approved by the Army Council and the King, are these:-

(i.) The general honour "South Africa" has been granted (a) to the three regiments of Household Cavalry, which sent a composite regiment to the war; (b) to any Yeomanry or Volunteer unit (including Colonial Volunteer units) which sent a contingent of 20 men or more; (c) otherwise, and apart from the above special cases, to any unit which fought as a unit in the war.

(ii.) In addition an authorized list of six "battle honours" has been compiled – Modder River, Paardeberg, Defence of Kimberley, Relief of Kimberley, Defence of Ladysmith, Relief of Ladysmith. Units, the headquarters of which, with at least half their strength, were present on any of those occasions, have received the appropriate distinction. Except that the composite regiment of Household Cavalry, when present at engagements in the strength stated, earned distinctions for all the three corps of which it was made up, no exemptions have been made from this rule in the case either of regular or auxiliary troops.

3.

The rules explained in the preceding paragraph are in accordance with the precedents set in the case of previous wars; and, up to now, alike in the case of both South African and of other wars, they have been applied to Colonial in the same manner as to Imperial troops. It is true that an exception occurred last year in the case of a Canadian unit, which the War Office allowed to bear the honour "Saskatchewan," although its headquarters had not been present at the engagement. This concession however was owing to the fact that the regiment had already been irregularly granted the distinction by a local mistake, and the late Secretary of State, in giving covering sanction, accepted the Adjutant-General's recommendation that the case must not form a precedent, and that the "Headquarters" and "50 per cent." rule should be strictly kept in future.

Departure from rules which is now proposed

4.

Now however the Cape Colony Government want to stretch the rules in two ways—

(a.) They want battle honours given to any Volunteer corps under their administration of which a company only was present at the engagement,

(b.) They want to add the following new battle honours to the authorized list – "Wepener," "Relief of Wepener," "Wittebergen."

5.

Similarly the Rhodesian Government ask for honours to be given in respect of the defence and relief of Mafeking, which they apparently think has been inadvertently overlooked.

6.

The difficulty about giving battle honours to corps not present with head-quarters and 50 per cent of their strength has been explained above.

There are also difficulties about enlarging the list of authorized battle honours. This list is based ultimately (in accordance with the usual practice) on the list of medal clasps awarded for the war, but with much condensation; out of 24 battle clasps six only (as above-mentioned) became battle honours, and the King, it should be noted, thought the condensation an improvement.

7.

It should further be observed (a) that whilst the additional battle honours now asked for by the South African Governments are all medal clasps except "Relief of Wepener," the Army Council have already definitely decided that "Wittebergen," at any rate, is not sufficiently important to be made an honour, and (b) that although the defences of Wepener and Mafeking were carried out practically by South African troops only, regular troops and oversea colonials took part in large numbers in the other operations, so that any grant of honours to the South African troops in respect of these might reopen the whole question of the award of honours.

Further questions raised by correspondence

8.

Apart from the above, the following miscellaneous points arising out of correspondence are for decision:–

(a) Whether the British South African Police (sic), which is now and normally a semi-military police force, is to be considered eligible (if otherwise qualified) for honorary distinctions in respect of its military service in the South African war.

(b) Whether the Natal Naval Corps (Militia) and Natal Field Artillery (Militia) are to be considered eligible. The Royal Navy and Regular Artillery do not receive honorary distinctions.

(c) Whether certain Natal militia units which served in the war as volunteer units, but have since been converted to militia, may be given the benefit of the less stringent conditions applicable to volunteers explained in paragraph 2 (i.) above.

(d) Whether the "First City (Grahamstown) Volunteers" may bear any honours earned in the war by "Marshall's Horse." It appears that Marshall's Horse was a temporary corps formed out of mounted troops drawn from the Grahamstown corps. The name was changed at the request of the Imperial military authorities, to avoid confusion with the City Imperial Volunteers.

9.

Lord Selbourne and the Colonial Office have no objection, on ground of policy, to the grant of honours to corps in South Africa.

General questions for decision

10.

The questions for decision are:-

(1) May any Cape Colony corps of which at least one company was present at any engagement qualifying for battle honours receive those battle honours; or must the ordinary "headquarters and 50 per cent." rule be enforced? Any special treatment will presumably have to extended to all other colonial corps.

(2) May any of the following:- "Defence of Wepener," "Relief of Wepener," "Wittebergen," "Defence of Mafeking," "Relief of Mafeking," be added to the authorized list of battle honours:–

(3) May any of the following corps, if qualified under the general rules, be granted honours:– British South Africa Police, Natal Naval Corps, Natal Field Artillery?

(4) May the Natal militia units which fought in the war as volunteers earn

the general honour "South Africa", under volunteer rules, i.e., if 20 men only of the corps were present?

(5) Whether the First City (Grahamstown) Volunteers may bear any honour earned in the war by "Marshall's Horse."

REGISTER No. 079 (Contd.)   **Minute Sheet No. 7**
AG. 1

This was decided by AG some time ago. It is not considered by him necessary to put this before the Army Council.

A letter should be drafted for his approval – saying that the Regulations as to grant of honours must be adhered to:

1. No.

2. No.

3. No. The British South Africa Police did not, it is understood, serve as a unit. The other Corps do not earn War honours. 'Ubique' covers all.

4. It is considered that Volunteers converted to Militia should carry with them their honours gained under Volunteer conditions – but the GOC SA should have a voice in this.

5. The Grahamstown City Volunteers should be allowed the honours of Marshall's Horse – subject to the approval of GOC SA.

23.08.06. Illegible Initials

SUBMISSION BY THE SECRETARY OF STATE FOR WAR TO KING GEORGE V

Mr. Amory, with his humble duty to the King, begs to submit for Your Majesty's approval the accompanying list of Great War Battle Honours claimed on behalf of the various units of the forces of Southern Rhodesia, as set out in the enclosed despatch from the Governor of Southern Rhodesia.

These claims have been checked by the War Office Battle Honours Committee, and the Army Council have concurred in the submission of the list for Your Majesty's approval.

ning Street,

4ᵗʰ May, 1925.

List of Battle Honours claimed on behalf of
various units of the forces of
Southern Rhodesia.
_____

1. The British South Africa Police.
   The Great War - 1 Battalion
   "E. Africa 1916-18"

2. The 1st Rhodesia Regiment.
   The Great War - 1 Battalion.
   "S.W.Africa 1914-15"

3. The 2nd Rhodesia Regiment.
   The Great War - 1 Battalion.
   "Kilimanjaro", "Behobeho", "E.Africa 1916-17".

4. The 1st Rhodesia Native Regiment.
   The Great War - 1 Battalion.
   "E.Africa 1916-18".

5. The 2nd Rhodesia Native Regiment.
   The Great War - 1 Battalion.
   "E.Africa 1917-18".

Colours presented by
His Most Gracious Majesty The King Emperor,
to the British South Africa Police in recognition of
Services rendered to the Empire in the South African War.
1899 - 1902.

A Colour Party, 1907.

BRITISH SOUTH AFRICA POLICE MEMORIALS

In the past, members of the Association have raised the subject of "the lack of a memorial" dedicated to the members of the British South Africa Police who have served the nation in many conflicts since their formation.

Before 2010 we did not have a dedicated Memorial but we shared one in good company with the rest of the British Commonwealth. The name "Cavalry Memorial" is itself a misnomer, the memorial has a wider compass, being dedicated to the "Mounted Forces of the Empire". The pre-WWII members of the Association would have remembered this as they were represented at the annual parade in May of each year.

The memorial was originally erected near Stanhope Gate in Hyde Park by public subscription, to commemorate the men of the Mounted Forces of the Empire who had served in WWI. After 1945, WWII was included and in 1975 the additional words "And on active service thereafter" were added. When Park Lane was widened the memorial was moved to the present location on South Carriage Road near the bandstand. The memorial consists of an impressive central figure of Saint George slaying the dragon mounted on a stone plinth, the background is a half circle stone surrounding wall on which are mounted bronze plaques listing the forces of each country commemorated. One plaque carries the words 'Mounted Forces of Southern Rhodesia'. The statue was created by Captain Adrian Jones and is cast from the metal of guns captured by the cavalry during WWI.

Dedication and unveiling of the memorial took place on the 21st May, 1924, in the presence of the Prince of Wales and the Duke of Connaught. On parade that day were members of all the mounted regiments of the Empire, the British South Africa Police being represented by Lieut. H.M. Surgey. There is nothing to confirm if he was on the parade with other members of the Regiment, I have had no success in locating a copy of *The Outpost* for 1924 and that I presume would have reported this event. The only record I have found connecting the Regiment to the parade is a line in Volume II, page 186, of the *History of the B.S.A.P.* Other sources, *The Times*, *Illustrated London News*, *Rhodesia Herald*, etc., have produced only general reports of this parade.

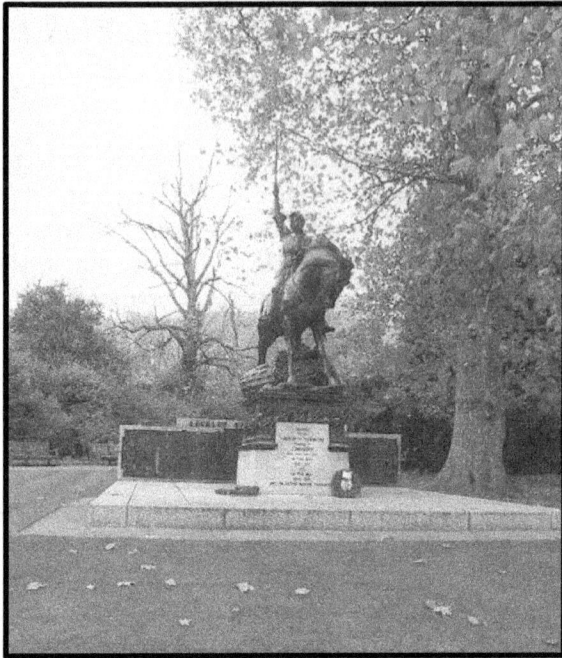

Front View: Cavalry Memorial, London.

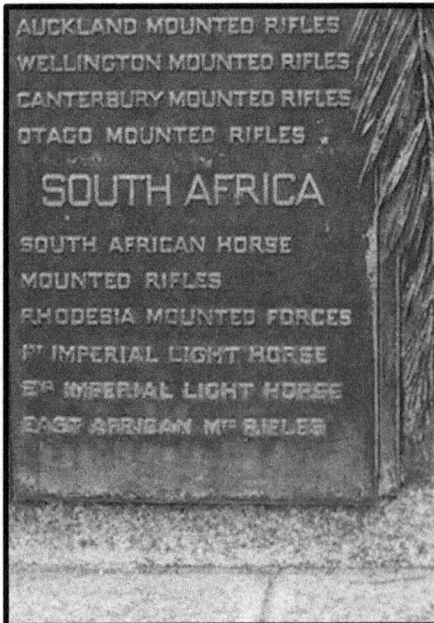

Rear View Detail: Plaque shows 'Rhodesia Mounted Forces'.

THE CAVALRY WAR MEMORIAL

UNVEILING ON WEDNESDAY

The Cavalry War Memorial at Stanhopegate, Hyde Park, will be unveiled on Wednesday by Field-Marshal Lord Ypres, and the Prince of Wales will place a large wreath upon it from all Cavalry Regiments of the British Empire.

For the memorial, Captain Adrian Jones, the sculptor, adopted the principle that the figure of the patron saint of the Cavalry arm, St. George, should be that not only of a saint but a knight as well, and the statue shows St. George, having broken his lance in subduing the dragon, reining in his charger and uplifting his sword as a signal that the enemy has been subdued. The most important feature of the statue is perhaps the cap-a-pied armour of St. George, this being the first time a complete statue in armour has been attempted in London. The committee received advice and criticism on this from Major Victor Farquharson and Sir H. Farnham-Burke, Garter King-at-Arms, and the armour shown is of the period of about 1460. Much of it is taken from the bronze effigy of the Earl of Warwick, while the arms, breast and back plates, the sword, spurs and gauntlets were all taken from rare pieces lent by Sir Henry Burke. The design of the horse and its furniture was adopted from the picture of St. George painted by Albert Durer in the 15th century. The panels surrounding the upper part of the plinth do not represent any particular drill-book formation but that of the assembly previous to formation, thus giving the opportunity of producing an artistic frieze, and also of commemorating soldiers of all the Cavalry regiments of the Empire in their fighting dress. On the background is a bronze plate commemorating the various units which made up the Empire cavalry in the war, and also recording that four cavalry officers were promoted Field-Marshal during the war. The bronze statue is cast from metal obtained from guns taken by the cavalry.

At the ceremony on Wednesday units serving abroad will be represented by detachments from the 1st and 2nd Lifeguards, Royal Horse Guards, 3/6th Dragoon Guards, 1st Royal Dragoons, 7th Queen's Own Hussars, 10th Royal Hussars, 12th Royal Lancers, 12/18th Hussars, 14/20th Hussars and 17/21st Lancers, regular cavalry regiments serving at home. There will also be a combined detachment from the 1st King's Dragoon Guards, the Queen's Bays (2nd Dragoon Guards), 4th Queen's Own Hussars, 11th Hussars, and the 15/19th Hussars. Besides these there will be detachments

124

representing the Royal Horse Artillery, The North Irish Horse, the British South Africa Police, 1st and 2nd Light Horse (Australia), the New Zealand Mounted Rifles, and a detachment comprising one officer and over 200 other ranks representing some 35 Yeomanry regiments (converted or otherwise).

(From a newspaper report)

The Blatherwick Memorial at the Police Depot in Salisbury

This Memorial was unveiled on the 30th of March, 1921, by Major General A.H.M. Edwards, Commissioner of the B.S.A.P. James Kincaid Blatherwick (Reg. No. 20) was one of the best known Regimental Sergeant Majors of the Police.

After service in the Bechuanaland Border Police, he joined the B.S.A.P. in 1896 and served during the Mashona and Matabele Rebellions and the Anglo-Boer War and was R.S.M. of the Police Contingent at the Coronation of 1911. He also took part in the Jameson Raid.

The British South Africa Police Memorial

On the 25th of July, 2010, the B.S.A.P. Memorial was unveiled at the National Memorial Arboretum, England, by Lord Walker, son of a former B.S.A.P. member, the late Colonel W.D.H. Walker (Reg. No. 3989). Nearly 400 ex-members and associates from all over the world attended the ceremony. The Memorial was modelled on the Blatherwick memorial, but with four bronze plaques, one on each face. These plaques are shown individually on the following pages. There was a poignant note to this ceremony in that while one of the first Commissioners of the B.S.A.P., General Edwards, unveiled the Blatherwick memorial, this unveiling was attended by the very last Commissioner of the B.S.A.P., Mr. P.K. Allum.

(Note: A transcription of the text on this plaque follows.)

BRITISH SOUTH AFRICA POLICE

In 1889 Cecil Rhodes negotiated a Royal Charter to occupy and explore the territory to the north of the present Republic of South Africa. The British South Africa Company Police was formed the same year and accompanied the first pioneer column, under the command of Lieutenant Colonel S.G. Pennefather, in its northern march from Mafeking to Mashonaland.

On 13th September of 1890, the Union Jack was raised at Fort Salisbury and thus was established the colony that was to become Southern Rhodesia, now Zimbabwe.

In 1896 the force became known as the British South Africa Police and developed as a light cavalry regiment with military Ranks and discipline. The regiment participated in the Matabele War (1893), the Jameson Raid (1895) and the Matabele and Mashona Rebellions (1896-7). The B.S.A.P. played an active role in the Boer War and later in campaigns in German East and South West Africa.

During these years two of its members were awarded the Victoria Cross. In 1904 King Edward VII conferred upon the B.S.A.P. the status of a Regiment and a Banner was presented in appreciation of services rendered during the Boer War.

In 1980 the British South Africa Police, in name, ceased to exist with the formation of Zimbabwe and the lowering of the Rhodesian national flag.

From 1889 to 1980 Members of the British South Africa Police served with distinction and honour in a Force with a great and proud tradition.

(NOTE: A transcription of the text on this plaque follows.)

BRITISH SOUTH AFRICA POLICE

Over the years from 1890 the unique character of the B.S.A.P. evolved and grew to influence and stabilise the rule of law over Rhodesia. Its members doubled as surveyors, road builders, telegraph linesmen, veterinary inspectors and were often the founders of the many tiny settlements that were to become thriving agricultural and mining districts.

In World War II the Force played a conspicuous part. Members served in East Africa, the Middle East, eastern Mediterranean, and many other theatres.

Members of the force were responsible for creating new police forces, in areas formerly occupied by the enemy.

After that war, and as the population of Southern Rhodesia rapidly expanded, the force became more specialised as Ballistics, Dogs, Forensic, Radio and Traffic expertise welded the Force into a highly successful and envied civil entity. The Criminal Investigation Department, in particular, was highly regarded throughout the western hemisphere.

The singular background of the B.S.A.P. enabled it to claim the privilege of 'standing to the right of the line' in parading with other forces of the Crown and as a respected, efficient and effective force it was on several occasions called to the assistance of neighbouring territories to quell civil unrest.

In 1954, Her Majesty Queen Elizabeth the Queen Mother consented to become the Honorary Commissioner of the British South Africa Police.

In the years from 1970, the B.S.A.P., together with other Rhodesian military units fought relentlessly in combating the infiltration of Communist trained terrorists and it was during those succeeding ten years that regular and reservist members served with honour, many giving their lives for their country.

PRO REGE   PRO LEGE   PRO PATRIA

B.S.A.P. Memorial photographs courtesy of Fred Punter (4853)

At the time of the unveiling of the Memorial, a Roll of Honour was also dedicated and laid up in the Chapel at the Arboretum. This Roll was a copy of the Roll of Honour of the British South Africa Police, printed, bound in leather and donated by Leslie Burrow (9591).

On the 28th July, 2013, an additional plaque was placed on the Memorial to commemorate the Centenary of the Regimental Association. A large number of former members attended and the plaque was unveiled by Major-General Pennefather, grandson of Lieutenant-Colonel Pennefather, who commanded the Pioneer Column in 1890.

'This Additional Plaque was Unveiled on 28th July 2013 to Commemorate the Centenary of the Formation of the B.S.A.P. Regimental Association"

At Fochabers, in Morayshire, Scotland, this Memorial was erected to the memory of the members of the Shangani Patrol. It is in the form of a drinking fountain in red and gray granite and is erected opposite the War Memorial and the main entrance to Gordon Castle.

The Inscription reads: "Erected by natives of Fochabers and others, to commemorate the heroic stand made against the Forces of the King of Matabeleland by Major Allan Wilson of this town who with a small band of gallant comrades fell bravely fighting against overwhelming odds near the Shangani River in South Africa on the 4th December, 1893'.

(Photographs courtesy of Michelle Frost and Fred Punter)

www.ingramcontent.com/pod-product-compliance
Lightning Source LLC
Chambersburg PA
CBHW060400090426
42734CB00011B/2209